IT'S ALL ABOUT

JESUS

THE LIVING WORD
VOLUME 2

31 **MORE** DEVOTIONS CONNECTING
EVERYDAY LIFE TO GOD'S WORD

DEBORAH BEDSON

Cover Design by 100Covers.com
Interior Design by FormattedBooks.com

ISBN: 978-1-7731812-3-5

DEDICATION

To Jesus Christ, my Lord and Savior, the Author and Finisher of my faith. Thank you for the divine guidance and inspiration I have received from You through the power of the Holy Spirit. May my humble attempt to bring Your Word into the hearts of the readers honor and glorify You.

GOING DEEPER

This book is meant to be used as a supplement to a regular Bible reading plan.

To dig deeper into God's Word and to make your study richer, it is recommended that you read each passage listed in its full context. That is, read the entire chapter the scripture is pulled from.

FREE RESOURCE

If you would like to have corresponding journal pages, you can download them for no charge at:

https://colossal-leader-3942.ck.page/6b5db1b4ed

You will receive a link to a PDF file.

Or you can contact us at:
itsallaboutjesusthelivingword@gmail.com

Happy studying, and may God increase your knowledge of His Word.

CONTENTS

INTRODUCTION

Hello, and welcome to "IT'S ALL ABOUT JESUS THE LIVING WORD" Volume 2. I am so happy that you have found your way here. Whether you are new to this series, or if you are joining me from Volume 1, my prayer is that you will draw closer to Jesus as you go along on this journey with me.

Volume 2 picks up right where volume 1 left off. Each day will deal with a common, hopefully relatable, story that I have observed or experienced. It is amazing when you dig into the Bible, how our everyday experiences can be found one way or another within the pages of scripture. You will find some humor, encouragement, and yes, conviction along the way. If we are not made a little uncomfortable, then we aren't growing, amen?

There are a couple additions to volume 2. A fourth question has been added to help you to connect with one of the passages studied that day. Then, a challenge at the end of each chapter, titled, "CALL TO ACTION". It is putting something you learned that day to work. Please don't skip over this part. It will help you grow, I promise!

I have often said, that while my name is listed as author on the cover, I really am just the transcriber. A topic is prompted by the Holy Spirit, and I sit down and write. The word comes from the Master Author and Finisher of our faith, Jesus Christ. So if you feel a personal connection to these topics, He is speaking to you. My prayer is that you will embrace whatever it is He wants to say to you. And just for the record, I felt some conviction along the way too!

Each devotional is set up to address a specific topic. A story is presented, with correlating scriptures and some brief comments for your consideration. There are 31 devotions. One can easily be completed in a day. Or, if you want to dig deeper into the passages, take a few days. The pace is entirely up to you.

HOW TO GET THE MOST OUT OF YOUR STUDY TIME:

1. Before you start, pray for God to give you understanding and new insights into His Word.
2. Read through the devotion.
3. Get a notebook and pen and jot down thoughts, impressions, and questions as you read the passages.
4. Go deeper into the study by looking up the scripture, and read the entire chapter it comes from, so you can understand the context.
5. Reflect on what you read, and consider your responses as you fill in the questions at the end of each devotional.
6. Consider how the devotional, and the scriptures specifically, speak to your personal experiences. Can you relate to the story? Have you had similar experiences or feelings?
7. Complete the Call to Action portion. Some days may be tougher than others, but it will help you to grow.

My disclaimer:

**I do not profess to be a theologian, Bible scholar, or even a teacher. I am a student of the Word, just as you are. It is my hope and prayer that we will together glean beautiful nuggets of truth about our glorious Savior. At the end of the day, we will see that it all boils down to this fact:

It's All About Jesus!

So grab your Bible and let's get started!

KAMIKAZE KITTY
(Reckless Abandon)

IF YOU READ MY FIRST devotional, you will remember that Day 1 began with a story about my sweet but fearful pooch named Levi. You know, those flies that drove him into hiding?

Well, I thought I would start this book with a story about our new cat, a sweet little thing I named Emma. She is the antithesis of Levi in just about every way. He was a dog; she is a cat. He was male; she is female. He ran from flies; she goes after them like a torpedo! When she spots a fly or a moth, she will zone in on it with pinpoint precision. And it doesn't matter what may be in the way between her and that bug. She has crashed through the window screen, flown right across the chicken wire that was protecting my little garden from her, and knocked pictures off a shelf, all in the name of her pursuit.

She is pretty much fearless. She loves to get into just about everything, and if things crash down around her, she doesn't run for cover, but stands there assessing the situation. Her curiosity has gotten her into a few jams. As a side note, she has a toilet paper fetish. She sees a roll and has got to claw it to shreds. I wasted money buying her toys. I guess I should have just bought her a package of Charmin!

Here is a scenario to ponder. If you saw your child running right out into the street, wouldn't you go after him or her with total abandon, not thinking of the consequences to yourself? Doesn't the idea of saving someone whom you love with all your heart outweigh the dangers you may encounter in your actions? I think most of us would disregard what might happen to ourselves but would run after them with reckless abandon in order to save them.

Going after things with a fearless, reckless heart reminds me of the love that we can and should have for our Lord Jesus. We need to have a love for Him that is so deep, we couldn't imagine our lives without Him. And we wouldn't care who knew it.

The Lord loves us with that total and complete abandon. A love so deep and profound it is immeasurable. Here are some scriptures to ponder:

HIS DEEP LOVE FOR US

"For God so loved the world that He gave His only begotten Son, that whoever believes in Him should not perish but have everlasting life." (John 3:16) To love us so much, in all our frailty, that He would give His only Son, is the ultimate act of sacrificial and deep love.

"Greater love has no one than this, than to lay down one's life for his friends." (John 15:13) Jesus willingly gave His life for us, it was not taken from Him.

"But God, who is rich in mercy, because of His great love with which He loved us, even when we were dead in trespasses, made us alive together with Christ." (Ephesians 2:4-5) A love that is so powerful, that because of it we are now alive in Him, freed from the curse of death caused by a sinful life.

"And we have known and believed the love that God has for us. God is love, and he who abides in love abides in God, and God in him." (1 John 4:16) When we truly love, we abide in each other, our hearts entwined. We become as one.

"The Lord has appeared of old to me, saying: 'Yes, I have loved you with an everlasting love; therefore, with lovingkindness I have drawn you.'" (Jeremiah

31:3) His love for us will never fade away. It is a sweet, enduring, tender yet fierce love.

HOW ARE WE TO LOVE IN RESPONSE?

"And you shall love the Lord your God with all your heart, with all your soul, with all your mind, and with all your strength. This is the first commandment." (Mark 12:30) We are to commit every part of our being to love Him-emotionally, physically, and spiritually. Even then, it is far less than He deserves.

"We love Him because He first loved us." (1 John 4:19) Because of this amazing love He has shown us, we are left with no other response than to love Him in return.

"For this is the love of God, that we keep His commandments; and His commandments are not burdensome." (1 John 5:3) We know that God only has the best for us, and we should respond with a joyous heart.

I find it so amazing that God would love me with such a fierce and unfailing love. The only response I can have is to love Him in return with the same abandon. The problem is we get caught up in a world view of love. It is hard to imagine that perfect love. Our measuring stick is our earthly relationships, where we have failed people, and where we have been let down. But let me reassure you that God's love is never-ending and never-failing. This is probably the best description in the Bible of what perfect love is:

"Love suffers long and is kind; love does not envy; love does not parade itself, is not puffed up; does not behave rudely, does not seek its own, is not provoked, thinks no evil; does not rejoice in iniquity, but rejoices in the truth; bears all things, believes all things, hopes all things, endures all things." (1 Corinthians 13:4-7) Wouldn't life be so much better if we were able to demonstrate this kind of love, not only to God but to one another?

REFLECTION TIME

How would you evaluate your love relationship with Jesus? Is it on fire, with a burning abandon, or has it grown a little cold?

_____

_____

_____

_____

After reading the passages above, how does knowing the depth of God's love increase your desire to love Him in return?

_____

_____

_____

_____

Choose one of the scriptures and discuss how it has touched and moved you to a closer relationship with Jesus. Commit it to memory.

_____

_____

_____

_____

Write a prayer asking God to show you how to love with abandon as He loves us.

_____

_____

_____

_____

Dear Heavenly Father:

Thank you, Lord, for first loving us. Especially when we can be such an unlovable bunch of people. Sometimes I can't help but wonder why You tolerate us. But we know that Your promises are true. You say in Your Word that You will never leave us nor forsake us. There is nothing that can separate us from Your love, whether it be death, life, height, depth, angels, principalities or any other created thing. That is powerful. I pray that we take this truth into our hearts, and in response demonstrate a genuine and abiding love that You so richly deserve. Thank you again for loving us, warts and all! In Your precious name, Amen!

CALL TO ACTION!

Marching orders:

Look at the scripture above, 1 Corinthians 13:4-7. Write out the scripture in your journal, but in every place where the word "love" is used, put your name there. List each description as a separate sentence. Step two is to honestly evaluate each sentence. Is this true about you? If yes, awesome! If the answer is no, oops! No worries. Step three is to take it to the Lord in prayer, ask for forgiveness, and to reveal how you can change that no to an honest yes. Step four-start applying His direction to you.

Ready, set, go!

THERE'S A WORM IN MY APPLE!
(Producing Good Fruit)

IMAGINE THIS SCENARIO. YOU PICK up a gorgeous looking piece of fruit. Let's say it's an apple. Luscious and red, just beautiful. You take a big bite. Crunch! Crispy and juicy. You take a second bite. The juice runs down your chin. You pause to examine your apple, and you notice something not so wonderful. There's a worm in it. Or worse yet, half a worm! (Sorry, I hope you have already eaten lunch.) What is your reaction? Most likely that apple goes in the trash or compost bin.

Up here in the Pacific Northwest, we have wild blackberries that grow everywhere. In fields, along the highways, they're invasive. But they produce very tempting fruit. The first summer here, we had blackberries growing in the field across the road from our house. We were tempted, so we gathered them by the bucketful. Of course, you tend to eat as you pick, right? But mama always said, wash your fruit before you eat it. She was right. We soaked the berries in a bowl of water. Sure enough, before long, these tiny worms floated to the top. Not very appetizing, that's for sure.

I went out to my garden one day to check on my tomatoes. At first glance, they looked perfect and ready to be washed and put right into the dinner salad. But after lifting a few vines, I was dismayed to find that the slugs had gotten to them before I did. What was beautiful on the outside, was rotten underneath. Totally useless.

The Bible speaks a lot about fruit, but with an entirely different meaning. It refers to the "produce" of our lives. In other words, it is the result of our hearts and actions as we live out our Christian lives. The seed that is planted is primarily the Word of God. When we live out the teaching of the Word, we produce good fruit. But if we continue in our sinful ways, still living in our flesh, then we produce bad fruit. Let's look at some scriptures:

JESUS THE VINE

"I am the vine, you are the branches. He who abides in Me, and I in him, bears much fruit; for without Me you can do nothing." (John 15:5) It all begins with our relationship with Jesus. We need to be completely grafted to Him, drawing our life-giving nutrients from Him.

"You will know them by their fruits. Do men gather grapes from thorn bushes or figs from thistles? Even so, every good tree bears good fruit, but a bad tree bears bad fruit. A good tree cannot bear bad fruit, nor can a bad tree bear good fruit. Every tree that does not bear good fruit is cut down and thrown into the fire. Therefore, by their fruits you will know them." (Matthew 7:16-20) While we are not called to judge people's hearts and motives, we are certainly told to recognize when someone is leading a fruitful life. It will also help us to discern whether someone is a false prophet. Always compare what people say to the Word of God.

LIVING A LIFE PLEASING TO HIM

"For this reason we also, since the day we heard it, do not cease to pray for you, and to ask that you may be filled with the knowledge of His will in all wisdom and spiritual understanding; that you may walk worthy of the Lord, fully pleasing Him, being fruitful in every good work and increasing in the knowledge of God." (Colossians 1:9-10). The apostle Paul was praying for the people of Colossae. We need to be filled with the Word in order to produce good fruit.

THE PARABLE OF THE SOWER

"Then He spoke many things to them in parables, saying: 'Behold, a sower went out to sow. And as he sowed, some seed fell by the wayside; and the birds came and devoured them. Some fell on stony places, where they did not have much earth; and they immediately sprang up because they had no depth of earth. But when the sun was up, they were scorched, and because they had no root they withered away. And some fell among thorns, and the thorns sprang up and choked them. But others fell on good ground and yielded a crop: some a hundredfold, some sixty, some thirty. He who has ears to hear, let him hear!'" (Matthew 13:3-9) In this parable, Jesus speaks of the Word of God going into our hearts. We can either have the seed penetrate deeply which will give us the ability to lead a fruitful life, or the seed can just bounce off a hard heart, making no positive impact at all.

"For you were once darkness, but now you are light in the Lord. Walk as children of light (for the fruit of the Spirit is in all goodness, righteousness, and truth)." (Ephesians 5:8-9) When we gave our lives to Jesus, the Holy Spirit indwelled in us. Because of this, we can live a life pleasing to God, therefore bearing good fruit.

THE FRUIT OF THE SPIRIT

"But the fruit of the Spirit is love, joy, peace, longsuffering, kindness, goodness, faithfulness, gentleness, self-control. Against such there is no law." (Galatians 5:22-23) This passage shows the opposite of living in the flesh. If we attain to exhibit these characteristics (and have them truly abiding in our hearts), we will have a bountiful harvest of good fruit to offer the Lord.

This life of following Jesus can be so rewarding, if we simply make the decision to please Jesus, abide in Him, and obey His Word. We can decide to just be content with being saved. But the deeds we do, not for salvation, but as a result of our salvation and our gratitude, will be rewarded. We can instead decide to give fully to Jesus and yield that hundredfold crop. And no worms!!

REFLECTION TIME

Have you desired to have a spiritual life that reaps a greater bounty? In what areas do you think you could improve? List them here.

_____

_____

_____

_____

What steps do you need to take to grow in the areas you have listed?

_____

_____

_____

_____

Look at the passage above about the Fruits of the Spirit. (Galatians 5:22-23) Commit it to memory. Where do you fall short, and what are your strengths?

_____

_____

_____

_____

Write a prayer asking God to help you to become stronger in the areas you are weak.

_____

_____

_____

_____

_____

Dear Heavenly Father:

Thank you that we can abide in you, just like the vine and the branches. We cannot exist in this walk without holding on to You, receiving our nourishment through Your Word every day. Help us to strive to live out the fruits of the Spirit, which will guard our hearts against the destructive acts of the flesh. Thank you for the empowering of the Holy Spirit. In your precious name, Amen!

CALL TO ACTION!

Marching orders:

Take a moment and journal down thoughts about the fruitfulness of your walk. Think about how much time you devote to reading God's Word. Not to just read academically, but to study, mediate and apply the Word. Develop an action plan, expanding on your answers to questions one and two.

Ready, set, go!

BUT I WANT IT!

(Needs Vs. Wants)

IF YOU ARE A PARENT, I am sure you can relate to this. Or, you might be having flashbacks to your own childhood antics.

When I was little, I would go to the store with my mom. It never failed, I always spotted something that I wanted and I just had to have it. Life itself would never be the same without this treasure. I would ask my mom for it. She usually said no, knowing that it was an impulse on my part. But I had a strategy that worked more often than not. I would pester her. And pester her. And pester her. I knew that if I could wear her down, she would eventually give in just to keep me quiet. In frustration, she would let me have it. I would be content for a while until it was all eaten, or broken, or I found something else I wanted even more!

Sadly, some adults never grow out of this mindset. That's what makes online shopping so dangerous. All you need to do is order your 'must have', whip out your credit card (so it doesn't even feel like you are paying for it) and wait for it to show up at your door. Look around your house. I bet you will find at least five things you bought that you can honestly say, "That was a waste of money!" I know I can.

I was in a store one time where this little girl was begging her mom for something. The mom leaned down so she was eye to eye with her, and gently asked her, "Is this a need or a want?" I don't think the item was purchased. I have tried this tactic with myself a few times. Then it becomes a battle of the flesh. I know I don't need it, Lord, but I want it.

We have a heavenly Father who wants to give us good gifts. But thankfully, He doesn't indulge our every whim. Thank goodness for that! He does promise to provide our needs. Check these passages:

"Do not fear, little flock, for it is your Father's good pleasure to give you the kingdom." (Luke 12:32) Wow! That sounds fabulous. An entire kingdom. But there is an expectation from the Lord on this. He wants us to put what we have been given to good use; not to indulge ourselves.

"And my God shall supply all your needs according to His riches in glory by Christ Jesus." (Philippians 4:19). Notice it says "need" not "want". That mom must have read this passage!

"And whatever things you ask in prayer, believing, you will receive." (Matthew 21:22) We must be careful how we apply this scripture. It is not an unqualified promise that all we have to do is believe and ask. When we ask things in prayer, we are always to be striving to be in God's will. He won't just give us things that are contrary to that.

"And whatever you ask in My name, that I will do, that the Father may be glorified in the Son. If you ask anything in My name, I will do it." (John 14:13-14). Be careful not to get into the trap of tacking on "In Jesus' name" to the end of your prayer to get what you want. Again, the key to answered prayer is being in the will of God.

THE DANGERS OF INDULGENCE

There is a very misleading and false doctrine today called the "Prosperity Gospel" or the "Word Faith Movement". This is the "Name it and claim it, blab it and grab it" crowd that teaches that God wants you to be rich, healthy, successful, etc. and all you need is to have enough faith. But if your prayers are not answered, or you are not healed, then the problem is that you are lacking in faith. The real problem here is that their teachings fly in the face of scripture. A very dangerous doctrine, indeed.

"Now godliness with contentment is great gain. For we brought nothing into this world, and it is certain we can carry nothing out. And having food and clothing, with these we shall be content. But those who desire to be rich fall into temptation and a snare, and into many foolish and harmful lusts which drown men in destruction and perdition. For the love of money is a root of all kinds of evil, for which some have strayed from the faith in their greediness, and pierced themselves through with many sorrows." (1 Timothy 6:6-10) If we walk in the truth of Jesus, He will give us the satisfaction we are seeking after.

"And He said to them, 'Take heed and beware of covetousness, for one's life does not consist in the abundance of the things he possesses.'" (Luke 12:15) Having an insatiable appetite for material things can lead us down a dangerous path.

"Do not lay up for yourselves treasures on earth, where moth and rust destroy and where thieves break in and steal; but lay up for yourselves treasures in heaven, where neither moth nor rust destroys and where thieves do not break in and steal. For where your treasure is, there your heart will be also." (Matthew 6:19-20) Earthly possessions will all eventually fade away. We need to be thinking about our heavenly treasures, which we can store up for future use. And they will be far more valuable than anything here.

There is nothing wrong with enjoying the things this earth provides. And sometimes God will bless us just because He can. But when we let our desires and impulses control us, or our possessions possess us, then we are getting into dangerous territory. The question we need to ask is this-does this truly satisfy, or are we seeking to satisfy some deep longing inside us? My guess is that as we grow deeper and deeper in our relationship with Jesus, those earthly desires will gradually diminish, and we will truly understand Paul's words "Godliness with contentment is great gain."

REFLECTION TIME

Think about one of those "I just have to have it" experiences. Did it truly satisfy, or did you crave the next new model?

_____

_____

_____

_____

As you grow in your walk with Jesus, are earthly desires diminishing, or are you still struggling with something?

_____

_____

_____

_____

Choose one of today's scriptures and memorize it. Explain below how you can apply it to your life.

_____

_____

_____

_____

Write out a prayer, committing your worldly desires to Jesus, and ask for them to diminish, and to fill those cravings with more of Him.

_____

_____

_____

_____

Dear Heavenly Father:

There are so many things in this world to catch our eye. The enemy is constantly flashing them before us, tempting us just like he did in the garden. Please do not allow us to succumb to those temptations, but to put earthly desires aside and seek more and more of You. We want to be content with a rich and full relationship with You that nothing on earth can compare to. Thank you. In Your precious name, Amen!

CALL TO ACTION!

Marching orders:

Go back to your answer to question #2. Think about that one thing that you feel you just can't live without. It could be very well that God is asking you to let go of it. Journal your thoughts about how it is occupying your time that could be better spent with Jesus. Ask Him to give you the strength to get rid of it. Pull it off like a band-aid. It hurts at first, but you will be ok! He will replace it with something better. I guarantee it.

Ready, set, go!

IT'S SIMPLE, BUT NOT EASY

(Following Jesus)

SIMPLE, BUT NOT EASY. IT sounds like a contradiction in terms, doesn't it? If you plug the word "simple" into your thesaurus search, the word "easy" pops right up. And the dictionary describes "simple" as "easy". So, if they mean virtually the same thing, then how can something be one but not the other?

Let me demonstrate that, despite what Webster thinks, we seem to live it every day. Have you ever tried to follow the written instructions on just about anything? The other day I tried to open a bottle of aspirin. You know, the ones with the childproof caps? "Push down and twist" it boldly told me. Since I am not a child, this should be a piece of cake, right? Wrong! I pushed, and pushed, grunted, and pushed some more. I looked at the cap with disdain and then tried again. After much pain to my hand, the cap finally came off. Victory! Not quite. Now there's the protectant seal I have to get off. Directions? Grasp tab and pull seal off. That microscopic tab that only a tweezer can grasp?? I don't think so. Instead, I grabbed a pair of scissors and stabbed a hole in it. Finally, I had access to the aspirin. But now my hand hurt too, and I think I cut myself with the scissors…..

When Jesus was building His team of disciples, He gave a "simple" directive. "Follow Me". Which they did. They left their jobs, families, and friends. It was a compelling request, and they did so willingly. These men were handpicked by the Messiah Himself. Two simple words. But was it easy? No. There were many challenges and hardships ahead.

THE COST OF DISCIPLESHIP

At the beginning of Jesus's ministry, He had many, many people who wanted to be His followers. But like most things, interest wanes, the "looky-loos" and the faint-of-heart drop off. Knowing this, and their hearts, Jesus challenged the followers in this conversation:

"Now it happened as they journeyed on the road, that someone said to Him, 'Lord, I will follow You wherever You go.' And Jesus said to him, 'Foxes have holes and birds of the air have nests, but the Son of Man has nowhere to lay His head.'

Then He said to another, 'Follow Me.' But he said, 'Lord, let me first go and bury my father.' Jesus said to him, 'Let the dead bury their own dead, but you go and preach the kingdom of God.'

And another also said, 'Lord, I will follow You, but let me first go and bid them farewell who are at my house.' But Jesus said to him, 'No one, having put his hand to the plow, and looking back, is fit for the kingdom of God.'" (Luke 9:57-62)

No doubt these responses weeded out more than a few people. So, what does Jesus ask of us when He beckons us to follow Him? Ponder these words:

"If anyone comes to Me and does not hate his father and mother, wife and children, brothers and sisters, yes, and his own life also, he cannot be My disciple. And whoever does not bear his cross and come after Me cannot be My disciple." (Luke 14:26-27) Jesus is not asking us to literally hate our family. But what He is asking is for us to love Him above all else.

"Then He said to them all, 'If anyone desires to come after Me, let him deny himself, and take up his cross daily, and follow Me.'" (Luke 9:23). What are we to deny ourselves? Our own desires, plans, worldly ways that are not in line with the life of Jesus. To take up our cross does NOT mean that we have

to endure some great hardship ("it's my cross to bear" some say.) But rather, to take those things that we are to deny, and totally surrender them to Jesus.

What are some of the things that we may be asked to surrender to follow Jesus? Anything that gets in between our relationship with Jesus needs to go. You may be asked to sacrifice a lot. But the gains will be worth it for sure!

We also can't follow Him when we try to lead. At work the other day, a customer asked one of the demo ladies where something was. She told him, and off he went. When she saw me, she yelled to the guy, "Follow the flower lady, she will show you where it is!" Well, he was already two aisles away. I said, "how can he follow me when I am back here?" How indeed can we follow Jesus when we keep wanting to get ahead of Him with our own ideas and plans? Aren't we then putting Jesus, whom we call Lord, behind us, thus making Him the follower? Not a good plan. We are to submit our desires to Him and be willing to follow His direction, even if it doesn't make sense.

"'For My thoughts are not your thoughts, nor are your ways My ways,' says the Lord. 'For as the heavens are higher than the earth, so are My ways higher than your ways, and My thoughts than your thoughts.'" (Isaiah 55:8-9) Boy, have I found that out to be true! But at the same time, I know that His ways are always going to be better than mine.

So here is the question. Are you willing to follow Jesus, knowing what the costs may be? Have you considered that you will have to give up things that you think you cannot live without? It's hard, but if we are truly going to follow Jesus, we must. But He is a gentleman. He never forced or coerced anyone to follow Him. He will ask, and let you decide. I pray you make the right decision!

REFLECTION TIME

When you made the decision to follow Jesus, what were some things that you had to "die to" in order to please Him?

_____

_____

_____

_____

Are there still some areas that you are struggling to let go of for His sake?

_____

_____

_____

_____

Which one of the scriptures in today's devotional struck a chord with you? Research it further. What have you learned from it?

_____

_____

_____

_____

Write out a prayer asking Jesus to show you what you need to let go of so you can follow Him more closely.

_____

_____

_____

_____

Dear Heavenly Father:

Thank You that You are calling us to Yourself. We recognize that although the command to follow You is simple, the actual task of doing so can be very difficult sometimes. But You never lead us into a direction that You will not provide what we need for the journey. There are many peaks and valleys, easy roads and treacherous ones. But help us to enjoy the journey, whether they be mountain top experiences or deep dark caverns. Because we know that no matter what, You are there beside us on this journey every step of the way. And what a glorious destination, when we finally see You face to face! In Your precious name, Amen!

CALL TO ACTION!

Marching orders:

Think about what the cost of following Jesus is, according to the scriptures we studied today. Have you truly considered them and what they mean to how you live your life now? In your journal, list five things that you feel you need to give up to truly surrender to Him. Give this some serious thought. Don't list superficial answers that don't have an impact. Make them count!

Ready, set, go!

STAYING ON THE RIGHT PATH
(The Straight and Narrow)

OUR FAMILY'S FAVORITE SUMMER VACATION was to go camping in Sequoia National Park. Lodgepole was the campground of choice. Every day we would take a different hike through the woods. One day, we decided to go on the very popular Congress trail. This is an easy, three-mile hike on a paved trail. Clearly marked for the tourist. Estimated time two hours. But that's not if you are the Bedson family.

We had a penchant for getting ourselves into little jams. As we were hiking along, we saw this humongous tree that had fallen across the meadow. This tree was big enough to walk across; so, we did. Then we decided to go a little further on a not-so-well marked trail. It also had many forks in it. I should caution the novice hiker that after a while, everything starts looking the same. We wandered here and there, beginning to feel like the Israelites in the desert. After hiking what seemed to be miles, we came across some other hikers who gave us directions back to the trail. All in all, what was supposed to be a two-hour hike turned into eight hours. (Is anyone else humming the Gilligan's Island theme song?) We were exhausted, and hungry. I can tell you we all slept well that night!

Roads and trails are marked to show us the correct way to go. If we get off course, we can get into a lot of trouble. Here's another story for you. Before we moved up to Washington from California, we did a "reconnaissance" trip to check out the area. We were on a tight schedule because we had pets and hotel reservations. As we were coming up highway 5 to our day's destination in Cottage Grove, Oregon, it was getting dark, but we had to press on to get to our hotel. As we traversed along the highway, we came across some road construction. They had the mountain road closed on one side (of course it was the inside lane of the highway). The lane was marked off on one side by the cement k-rails, and then the other side by orange trash can-sized cones. It was narrower than usual and seemed pitch black as the mountain area gets at night. I was driving, and let me tell you, it was a white-knuckle ride. I was holding onto the steering wheel for dear life! I just knew that if I got too close to the inside edge I would crash into the rails, or too close to the outside and I would go off the mountain. I am sure I had about fifty cars trailing behind me. I can hear you asking, "Why didn't you just use the car in front of you for a guide?" First off, what if he can't see either and goes off the edge? Secondly, I was going so slow that the gap between us was getting bigger and bigger! Anyways, I was praying all the way. The drive seemed endless. We eventually made it safely to our destination. I found out later that was a thirteen mile stretch of road construction. It's a good thing I didn't know it at the time!

The Bible speaks of the road to heaven.

"Enter by the narrow gate; for wide is the gate and broad is the way that leads to destruction, and there are many who go in by it. Because narrow is the gate and difficult is the way which leads to life, and there are few who find it." (Matthew 7:13-14)

THE ROAD TO DESTRUCTION

The path is wide, and the gate is easy to find. The masses can move through it with ease. How do we do that spiritually? We live with no regard to the teachings of Jesus, we engage in sinful practices, we listen to the false teachings that tell us all roads lead to heaven, love wins out, I'm a good person, etc. and we simply follow the crowd. It is an easy path that we can stroll down because it doesn't require any sacrifice on our part. We live the life WE choose. That is the fastest way down the slippery slope of destruction.

THE ROAD TO EVERLASTING

Jesus tells us the road to heaven is hard and the gate is narrow. It is not easy to live the Christian life. We must make sacrifices and hard decisions. We also have an adversary whose mission is to destroy us and take us down with him. Following Jesus requires a daily, even a moment-to- moment commitment to follow Him.

"Only be strong and very courageous, that you may observe to do according to all the law which Moses My servant commanded you; do not turn from it to the right hand or to the left, that you may prosper wherever you go." (Joshua 1:7) This was direction the Lord gave to Joshua when He gave him the command over the Israelites. If we keep our eyes on Jesus and follow His Word, we will be ok!

In my stories above, I shared two different pathways. The first, we wandered off on our own, ignoring the signs, letting our curiosity get the best of us. We got lost in broad daylight. In the second story, I was completely in the dark, with only my headlights to guide me and keep me on the road. But what got us safely through that was a deep and passionate clinging to Jesus, praying for Him to guide us along the way. The first path was easy, but wrong. The second one was gut-wrenching, but because I kept my eyes on Jesus, He saw us through. As He always does!

REFLECTION TIME

Think of a time when temptation led you on the wrong path. What was that like, and what was the cost?

_____

_____

_____

_____

Think of another time when you were tempted to stray from your path with Jesus. How did He keep you on your path?

_____

_____

_____

_____

Read Matthew 7:13-14 and commit it to memory. How would you use this scripture to exhort someone to stay on the right path?

_____

_____

_____

_____

Write out a prayer asking the Lord to help you to walk "the straight and narrow", and to give you the strength to resist following the crowd, but to keep your eyes on Him.

_____

_____

_____

_____

Dear Heavenly Father:

There is so much in this world competing for our attention. If we are not careful, we can get caught up in destructive actions and behaviors. Help us to be in constant fellowship with You, seeking Your face, so that when something comes along that could derail us and get us on the wrong path, we would be so closely bound to You that we cannot stray. Thank You that You promise You will never leave us nor forsake us. We want to have that same commitment to You. In Your strong name, Amen!

CALL TO ACTION!

Marching orders:

Think about where you currently are on your path with Jesus. Are you being tempted to stray, because something looks more enticing, or maybe this road is sometimes just too hard and you want to give up? Or at least take a break. Write down your thoughts in your journal. And be honest; God already knows your heart! Meditate on Joshua 1:7 and use God's Word to strengthen you and keep you on the straight and narrow.

Ready, set, go!

BADGE OF GRACE
(God's Daily Blessings)

IN 2005, THERE WAS AN outbreak of a staph infection, called MRSA, which is strongly resistant to antibiotics. It was dubbed a "superbug". It is highly contagious, and quick moving. Many people lost their lives, or at the least, limbs due to the infection. One lady who had previously attended our church contracted the infection. Within a period of three days, she went from being healthy to having her entire leg amputated.

I have been fortunate in my life that most of my health problems have been restricted to annual bouts of bronchitis. Aside from the childhood infections, and flu viruses that went around my school. Back then, it was almost a given that you never left the doctor's office without an injection and a prescription. We were pumped full of antibiotics. In 2005, I developed a sore, which looked like a boil on the back of my upper left leg. I tried every home remedy I could think of to heal it. My then-roommate kept telling me I needed to go see a doctor. But with no insurance or money, I thought I could take care of it. One day, I thought it was draining and getting better but instead it was abscessing. I was taking my mom to the doctor that next day, so I made an appointment for myself. We were joking around about something, laughing, until he saw my leg. He took one look and freaked out! That's not a reaction you want from your doctor. I immediately thought, well I am not getting out of here with just a prescription. It turned out that he had just lost a patient to MRSA the previous week. Before the day was over, I landed in the emergency room, and ended up with a hole that half a boiled egg could sit in. It took about 6 weeks to completely heal. I still have a nice scar on the back of my leg that occasionally itches or stings.

I have often wondered why God spared my life, or even my leg when people were dying from this. I call the scar on my leg my "badge of grace". Because it was God's grace that spared me. I am sure you have heard of incidences where one house in an entire neighborhood was left undamaged while everyone else's house was either burned down or demolished by a tornado. Why does God spare some, but not others? Why does He heal one person, but not another? Why does He seemingly bestow grace on your friend, but you are left to suffer?

That's a tough question to answer, and one that scholars far more knowledgeable than me have not been able to come up with a satisfactory answer.

I do know this: God's grace is amazing, God's ways are unfathomable, and I don't think we could fully comprehend the answer to the "why" question this side of heaven. And when we get to heaven, I don't think we are going to care.

WHAT EXACTLY IS GRACE?

Grace is a word that is tossed around quite a bit by Christians. Biblical grace is God blessing us when we are so undeserving of it. It is also an essential ingredient to our salvation.

"For by grace you have been saved through faith, and that not of yourselves; it is the gift of God, not of works, lest anyone should boast." (Ephesians 2:8-9) Our salvation is purely from God, and we can do nothing to earn it.

"Concerning this thing I pleaded with the Lord three times that it might depart from me. And He said to me, 'My grace is sufficient for you, for My strength is made perfect in weakness.' Therefore, most gladly I will rather boast in my infirmities, that the power of Christ may rest upon me." (2 Corinthians 12:8-9) Paul suffered from an undisclosed physical ailment. But rather than healing

him from it, God chose to give him the strength to endure it. And God was glorified through it. His grace was demonstrated.

"But by the grace of God I am what I am, and His grace toward me was not in vain; but I labored more abundantly than they all, yet not I, but the grace of God which was with me." (1 Corinthians 15:10) Paul, in his early days, was a full-blown Pharisee, a hater of Jesus. But because of God's grace, he was converted, and became one of the greatest ambassadors for the Christian faith that ever walked the earth. God has a purpose for each of us.

"As each one has received a gift, minister it to one another, as good stewards of the manifold grace of God." (1 Peter 4:10) Manifold means numerous or varied. And as the body of Christ, we are to use these different gifts to edify each other. We are not to hide them or use them for our own benefit.

"For we do not have a High Priest who cannot sympathize with our weaknesses, but was in all points tempted as we are, yet without sin. Let us therefore come boldly to the throne of grace, that we may obtain mercy and find grace to help in time of need." (Hebrews 4:16) Jesus knows everything we have experienced, every fear, every trial. So we can come boldly and directly to the throne (made possible by His death and resurrection) and lay out our hearts to Him. There is no other religion that can boast that!

God extends us grace and mercy for several reasons. He may have a purpose He wants to work through us, we have an opportunity to use the situation to share the love of Jesus, or He may want to teach us something from it. Whatever the reason, we need to be able to recognize when God has bestowed grace upon us. If we don't see the hand of God in it, or there is no call to discipleship, to repentance, or recognition of the redemptive work of the cross, then what we have is cheap grace. And believe me, the sacrifice and suffering that Jesus experienced on the cross was anything but cheap. It cost Him His life.

REFLECTION TIME

Think of an experience you once had where you believe God extended His grace to you. Discuss it here:

_____

_____

_____

_____

Can you relate to Paul's comments about God's grace being sufficient in his weakness? How would that strengthen you in your situation if that was the answer to your prayer?

_____

_____

_____

_____

Choose one of the scriptures in today's devotional and commit it to memory. How does this one speak to you?

_____

_____

_____

_____

Write out a prayer, asking God to intercede in an area that you need His grace.

_____

_____

_____

_____

Dear Heavenly Father:

Thank You for Your infinite gift of grace. Thank You that we cannot earn it but that You bestow it freely because You love us. Help us to recognize when You have extended Your grace, so that we can in turn share it with others to bless them. You are a good, good Father who desires to love and nurture Your children. That is so awesome! May we never take that for granted. In Your precious name, Amen!

CALL TO ACTION!

Marching orders:

Think about the "badge of grace" God gave to you in your answer to question #1. Why do you think He spared you the fallout from the situation? How can you use that to minister to someone else? Take a moment and think about someone that you need to extend some grace to. Pray about it, and ask God to show you how to implement that practically, and then put feet to it and do it!

Ready, set, go!

GOOGLE IT, PAT
(God's Word is Always Current)

WE LIVE IN A HIGHLY technological society. Everything seems to be linked to our computers, cell phones, or iPad. Do you remember when a phone was just that-a way to call and speak to a person? Now, phones can practically do anything.

Back in the 1990s when the internet became the latest thing, we were suddenly driving on the "information superhighway". Communicating via email or texting has replaced pen and paper. Information can be found in a matter of seconds through high-speed internet.

While our society depends on technology to do just about everything, not everyone has embraced it. Take my sister, Pat. She is a holdout from the good old days of pre-technology. She was dragged kicking and screaming into the 21st century, finally giving in and buying a cell phone. While most people are racing down the superhighway, Pat prefers to meander down a country road. She likes the slower pace of life. She uses reference books for information, a map for directions, and likes to talk to someone on the phone rather than text. At a former job, when she would ask a coworker about something, the common response was, "Google it, Pat".

While I spend a lot of time on my computer, I can relate to some of the older ways of doing things. I would much rather hold a book in my hands than read it on a device. And I enjoy hand-written Christmas letters rather than a mass email.

As handy as the fingertip-ready resource is, there is a drawback. The information is only as accurate as the person inputting it. Have you noticed that what was said yesterday and touted as fact, is now turned on its ear, and the opposite is said to be true? How do you know what to believe? And the latest buzz word is "fact-checker", touted by the last presidential campaigns. My only question is this- who is fact-checking the fact-checkers??

There is one certainty we can always rely on as fact. It is the immutable, unchanging Word of God. It means the same today as it did when it was written.

"Heaven and earth will pass away, but My words will never pass away." (Matthew 24:35) Jesus has just described what will happen during the Tribulation and His second coming. Although everything else is coming under destruction, God's Word will stand.

"For assuredly, I say to you, till heaven and earth pass away, one jot or one tittle will by no means pass from the law till all is fulfilled." (Matthew 5:18) For you Bible students, a jot and tittle are references to the Hebrew language. A jot is the 10th letter of the Hebrew alphabet and the smallest. A tittle is a tiny pen stroke that differentiates between 2 different letters. The emphasis here is that even the smallest letter of the law will be fulfilled.

"...The grass withers and its flower falls away, but the word of the Lord endures forever." (1 Peter 1:24-25) God's Word will never die.

"Forever, O Lord, Your Word is settled in heaven." (Psalm 119:89) God said it, and that settles it!

"All Scripture is given by inspiration of God, and is profitable for doctrine, for reproof, for correction, for instruction in righteousness, that the man of God may be complete, thoroughly equipped for every good work." (2 Timothy

3:16-17) People often dispute the Word of God as being written by man. But it clearly says here that it came from God Himself.

Another ongoing debate is the "cultural relevance" of God's Word. The argument by the liberal churches and the false doctrines is that God's Word is outdated and doesn't fit into the norms of today's society. To address all people, it is suggested we change or eliminate certain points to be sensitive to everyone, or to be "politically correct". In other words, we need to adapt God's Word to fit the times we are living in. Well, in my humble opinion, being both politically correct and Biblically correct doesn't fly. It's like trying to go two different directions at the same time because you have a left foot and a right foot. Give it a try, I dare you! God is very clear-sin is sin, whether it happened 2,000 years ago, or yesterday. And just because you haven't been struck down by lightning, it doesn't mean that God is ok with it. His grace allows for a change of heart, but if no change comes, there will be repercussions for that unrepentant heart.

"For the word of God is living and powerful, and sharper than any two-edged sword, piercing even to the division of soul and spirit, and of joints and marrow, and is a discerner of the thoughts and intents of the heart." (Hebrews 4:12). Wow! God's Word is alive! It has withstood the test of time and is always there to penetrate our hearts. (But not like the creature in the movie *Alien!*) It is there to transform restore, purify and cleanse us from all evil.

So in conclusion, whether you are a true techie, loving the latest gadget out there, or like my sister Pat, happy to stroll along, we can rest assured that no matter what the world throws at us, we can always take God's Word to the bank.

"Your Word I have hidden in my heart, that I might not sin against You." (Psalm 119:11) Study His Word, learn His truth, and live a life that is pleasing to Him.

REFLECTION TIME

Take a moment and reflect on how today's culture lines up with the Bible. Contrast the differences and similarities that you see.

_____

_____

_____

_____

Have you wrestled with what the world is telling you as fact, and what God's Word says? Share your experience and how you reconciled it.

_____

_____

_____

_____

If someone were to challenge you on the accuracy of God's Word in light of today's culture and "advanced" knowledge, what would be your response? Are your adequately equipped to answer them Biblically?

_____

_____

_____

_____

Write a prayer, asking God to reveal the truth of His Word, and to equip you with the ability to discern between truth and the lies of the enemy.

_____

_____

_____

_____

Dear Heavenly Father:

It is so difficult sometimes to separate truth from lies. But Your Word is very clear. Help us to stay focused on You, and not be swayed by the enemy to believe the "latest discovery" or to be caught up in the sinful lifestyles that have become an accepted part of our culture. Your truth has not changed since the day You spoke the world into existence, and it will remain until You come back to make things right. Your commandments are not popular with today's society. Give us the strength to stand firm in all adversity. In Your strong name, Amen!

CALL TO ACTION!

Marching orders:

Have you ever encountered someone who claims the Bible is irrelevant, outdated, not accurate? Take some time and prepare your thoughts to answer that person's objections to the Word. Always be ready to give a defense to everyone who asks you a reason for the hope that is in you, with meekness and fear; be armed with the truth, but always in love.

Ready, set, go!

EYES FRONT, PEOPLE

(Keep Your Eyes on Jesus)

I HAVE A PET PEEVE when I am watching an action movie. Why is it that when the girl is being chased, she keeps turning to look behind her? Doesn't she realize that slows her down? (Oops, she just lost her balance and twisted her ankle! Darn those six-inch heels.) When you are at a track meet, you will notice that the runners have their heads down and are focused on what is ahead of them, not behind them.

While I am on the subject of television, I get annoyed when the character does something dumb. I happened to be channel surfing recently and came across the movie "Godzilla". The original American one. Back then, the filming was cheesy. But as this monster was stomping through Manhattan, people kept stopping and looking around, or running in the same direction as the monster was going. Surely, they should have realized that he could easily outrun them. I thought to myself, just turn left down one of the streets. And for goodness sake, why are you following everyone down the subway stairs even though you hear him coming?? Or how about at the end of "The Birds", an old Alfred Hitchcock movie. Spoiler alert** After seeing the town terrorized for days by these birds, attacking and killing people all around her, our heroine hears them up in the attic of the house she is hiding in. For some unexplained reason, she is drawn up the stairs to where these killer birds are, and she is getting ready to open the attic door. At this point, I am rooting for the birds!!

I guess it is human nature to look all around us and get distracted by our surroundings. It amazes me how people blindly follow other people, without using an ounce of common sense. No wonder God compares us to sheep. That is exactly what they do.

Our adversary, Satan, knows this very well. So he devises all kinds of schemes to get our eyes off Jesus. He will distract us, entice us, and lie to us. He has been doing it since the garden of Eden.

"Now the serpent was more cunning than any beast of the field which the Lord God had made. And he said to the woman, "Has God indeed said, 'You shall not eat of every tree of the garden?'" (Genesis 3:1) Notice his first tactic. He placed doubt in her heart about what God has said. It was effective, and he has been doing that ever since.

"But I fear, lest somehow, as the serpent deceived Eve by his craftiness, so your minds may be corrupted from the simplicity that is in Christ." (2 Corinthians 11:3) History has been hard on Eve. If we were honest, we would have to admit we have been deceived by people far less cunning than Satan.

Satan has many other tactics, as well to distract us. He is the father of lies.

"You are of your father the devil, and the desires of your father you want to do. He was a murderer from the beginning, and does not stand in the truth, because there is no truth in him. When he speaks a lie, he speaks from his own resources, for he is a liar and the father of it." (John 8:44). It is important to know that Satan is incapable of truth. Every word that proceeds from his mouth is a lie. The only truth is that of Jesus Christ.

So how do we protect ourselves, and keep our eyes on Jesus?

"You will keep him in perfect peace, whose mind is stayed on You, because he trusts in You." (Isaiah 26:3) Keeping our eyes and minds on Jesus will give us peace in any storm. It will also keep us from being distracted. It's very hard to concentrate on two things at the same time.

"Let your eyes look straight ahead, and your eyelids look right before you." (Proverbs 4:25) Don't turn aside to sin and deceitfulness.

"I have taught you in the way of wisdom; I have led you in right paths. When you walk, your steps will not be hindered, and when you run, you will not stumble." (Proverbs 4:11-12). If we follow in the path of righteousness, we will not be stumbled by the world around us.

"Only be strong and very courageous, that you may observe to do according to all the law which Moses My servant commanded you; do not turn from it to the right hand or to the left, that you may prosper wherever you go. This Book of the Law shall not depart from your mouth, but you shall meditate in it day and night, that you may observe to do according to all that is written in it. For then you will make your way prosperous, and then you will have good success." (Joshua 1:7-8) God has just turned over the leadership of the Israelites to Joshua after Moses had died. He was giving him his marching orders. This is advice I think we can all use. But prosperity and success in God's economy, not ours. They often look completely different!

"Finally, my brethren, be strong in the Lord and in the power of His might. Put on the whole armor of God, that you may be able to stand against the wiles of the devil. For we do not wrestle against flesh and blood, but against principalities, against powers, against the rulers of the darkness of this age, against spiritual hosts of wickedness in the heavenly places. Therefore, take up the whole armor of God, that you may be able to withstand in the evil day, and having done all, to stand." (Ephesians 6:10-13) I would exhort and challenge all believers to read this passage every morning before we get out of bed. Putting on the armor is our best defense against the wiles of the devil.

In order to walk the right path with Jesus, we must keep our eyes on Him. We cannot let ourselves be distracted by anything the world or Satan may try to throw at us. Remember this:

"You are of God, little children, and have overcome them, because He Who is in you is greater than he who is in the world." (1 John 4:4)

REFLECTION TIME

As we discussed, Satan has many tactics to get our eyes off Jesus. Name one or two that he uses with you.

_____

_____

_____

_____

Now that you have identified your "weak spots", what are some ways that Satan can be neutralized in these areas of your life?

_____

_____

_____

_____

Take some time to study and memorize the passage in Ephesians 6:10-18. How can each piece of armor protect you?

_____

_____

_____

_____

Write a prayer asking God to help you keep your eyes focused on Him, and to protect you from the tactics of the enemy.

_____

_____

_____

_____

Dear Jesus:

Thank You for Your guidance on the path of righteousness. Thank You that You can help us to stay on the straight path, and not wander off here and there, looking in every direction but towards You. We have the truth of Your Word that will protect us from all of Satan's deceitful tactics. Your promise that You are always with us gives us great peace and comfort.

In Your precious name, Amen!

CALL TO ACTION!

Marching orders:

Refer to your answer to question #3. Research how each piece of armor will protect you. Come up with a game plan to strengthen the areas where you feel vulnerable. (Hint ~check out scriptures related to each "piece".)

Ready, set, go!

A ROSE IS A ROSE-OUCH!

(God's Pruning)

IN MY CURRENT JOB AS a floral merchandiser, one of my main responsibilities is to ensure the flowers are in tip-top shape. This requires a lot of daily maintenance. A specific task is to "groom" the roses, which entails pulling off the guard petals. These are the petals that form first on the rosebud, and their job is to do exactly what they are named for-to guard the rose before it is ready to bloom.

Sometimes these guard petals add a nice contrast in color to the full rose bloom. But often, as the flower develops, they turn a bit brown and detract from the beauty of the rose. Some people may look at them and think the rose is dying.

So it is Debbie to the rescue! This requires a gentle touch, lest you break the head. You hold the bud securely in one hand, and with your other hand you put your thumb at the base of the petal and pull it off. There are usually two, sometimes three, of these petals. When you are done, you have a fresh, beautiful rose. It can be tedious when you have twenty-four roses to a bouquet, and thirty bouquets on display, but the finished product is worth the effort.

If you have ever gardened, you have experienced the same thing. You weed, mulch, prune, feed. You want to give your plants every opportunity to yield healthy, strong flowers or produce. But there is a tricky side to this. Oh, the thorns. I can't tell you how many times I have been jabbed by those nasty little things. I was speaking with a friend of mine at church about this topic. We were discussing how God prunes us to reshape and refine us and comparing it to my job. I remember thinking, but if I am doing the pruning, why is it I am the one getting stuck with the thorns; yet when He prunes me, I am still the one feeling the pruning?

Wait a minute! Back the truck up, girl! Before we discuss pruning any farther, let's address the thorn issue. Am I really suggesting that Jesus doesn't know what the thorns feel like?? Am I daring to think that my little pricks can even come close to what He endured for me while preparing for the cross? Think back to when Jesus was being put on trial before His crucifixion. The Roman soldiers mocked Him:

"When they had twisted a crown of thorns, they put it on His head, and a reed in His right hand. And they bowed the knee before Him and mocked Him, saying, 'Hail, King of the Jews!'" (Matthew 27:29). When they put the crown of thorns on his head, they didn't just gently lay it there, they pressed it into his skull, causing extreme pain and bleeding. While they may have thought they were being funny, in reality these Roman soldiers were fulfilling Bible prophecy:

"But He was wounded for our transgressions, He was bruised for our iniquities" (Isaiah 53:5). Jesus, who was without sin, took on this punishment for us so that we can be made righteous.

Some commentators suggest that this crown of thorns was representative of the curse that came upon the earth following the sin of Adam and Eve: *"Both thorns and thistles it shall bring forth for you..."* (Genesis 3:18) No thorns existed before the fall.

Getting back to the discussion of pruning. What exactly is pruning? It is the removal of dead, overgrown branches or twigs that inhibit the growth of healthy new limbs, or it is removing branches or leaves that draw the energy of the plant into vines instead of the fruit, vegetable or flower.

Biblical pruning is essentially the same thing. God is taking away the sin and dead branches of our lives, cleaning us up so we can produce more fruit in our walk. Yes, like the thorns, it can be painful at times. But God never wants to inflict needless suffering on us. He always has a purpose for everything He does in our lives.

"Every branch in Me that does not bear fruit He takes away; and every branch that bears fruit He prunes, that it may bear more fruit." (John 15:2) God wants to clear away anything in our lives that hinders our walk with Him. So He removes the gunk, and nurtures and tends to the vines that are producing fruit to make us more Christ-like.

Abiding in the True Vine

"I am the vine; you are the branches. He who abides in Me, and I in him, bears much fruit; for without Me you can do nothing. If anyone does not abide in Me, he is cast out as a branch and is withered; and they gather them and throw them into the fire, and they are burned." (John 15:5-6) What does it mean to abide in Him? It is to have a genuine, intimate relationship with Him. We want to be so dependent on Him, that we are truly connected to Him. He is our lifeblood, our very sustenance.

"As the Father loved Me, I also have loved you; abide in My love. If you keep My commandments, you will abide in My love, just as I have kept My Father's commandments and abide in His love." (John 15:9-10) What an awesome thought that we can share the same deep love with Jesus that He has with His Father.

"Whoever confesses that Jesus is the Son of God, God abides in him, and he in God. And we have known and believed the love that God has for us. God is love, and he who abides in love abides in God, and God in him." (1 John 4:15-16) When we become believers in Jesus Christ, we become intertwined with Him.

"Take away the dross from silver, and it will go to the silversmith for jewelry." (Proverbs 25:4) Dross is the impurities that are found in gold and silver. When they fire it up, the dross is removed, leaving pure silver or gold. Jesus will remove the dross from our lives to make us pure.

Pruning can be painful at times. The cutting away of the sinful flesh in our hearts, removing things from our lives that pull us away from God is needful to give us a fruitful life. Like removing a splinter- it may hurt at the time, but it is necessary for our spiritual health. To abide in Jesus is to truly have that fruitful life.

REFLECTION TIME

Think of a time when God has done some pruning in your life. What was that like, and how did it change your relationship with Him?

_____

_____

_____

_____

Take a moment and think about what it means to abide in Christ. How can you draw closer to Him?

_____

_____

_____

_____

Review the scriptures discussed today. Choose one to commit to memory. How does it speak to you?

_____

_____

_____

_____

Write a prayer asking God to reveal to you anything in your life that needs to be pruned and to help you release it to Him.

_____

_____

_____

_____

Dear Heavenly Father:

Thank You that You love us with such a deep love, and that You want us to abide in You. We want to be so close to You that we can feel Your very heartbeat. Help us to willingly let go of the dross that resides in our life, and purify us. We can never be worthy of such a deep love, but we are so thankful that You give that to us. Pure grace, to be sure! In Your precious name, Amen!

CALL TO ACTION!

Get your journal out. In the prayer question, you were asked to seek the Lord for areas that need pruning. Make a list of what He says to You. If He hasn't revealed anything yet, ask more fervently! We ALL need pruning! Then start working on how you are going to let go of these areas, and how you will replace them with things of God. I challenge you to come up with five things.

Ready, set, go!

A TALE OF THREE BEANS

(Being Fruitful at Any Stage)

THERE ARE MANY PARALLELS BETWEEN the gardening world and human nature. Let me share this story of how three green bean plants responded to their circumstances.

BEAN PLANT #1

This plant was purchased at the end of the season. We thought it was quite a bargain at six plants for 75 cents! Wow, what a deal, right? Wrong. Remember that adage, "you get what you pay for"? These poor little guys had been left too long in the pot. Their roots were totally pot bound. Also, there was a serious lack of soil in the pot. At this stage, they were already halfway through their normal seasonal lifespan. The flowers were in bloom. These conditions resulted in stunted growth and a small harvest, yet there was still an effort put out by the plant to produce.

BEAN PLANT #2

These were plants that started by seeds. They were planted in the proper soil and received adequate sunlight and water. Unfortunately, snails and slugs came in and chomped off almost all the plant heads in their early seedling stage. However, when the bugs were controlled, they bounced back and grew to be healthy plants. A nice harvest was the result, albeit not what could have been if it hadn't been for the bugs.

BEAN PLANT #3

Now, these plants had the best circumstances. Great dirt, proper sunshine, water and NO BUGS! Yay! Under these conditions, they were able to flourish and as a result had a large, bountiful harvest. It lasted through the summer, and even into the beginning of Fall. Finally, they succumbed to the change of the season, and stopped producing fruit. The plants eventually died off.

These three scenarios each demonstrate a different level of being fruitful. Their circumstances were different, so the end-result was different as well. This is an illustration about how God will give each one of us unique gifts, talents, and opportunities. Some will have an easy road, while others will experience struggles and hardships along the way.

"As each one has received a gift, minister it to one another, as good stewards of the manifold grace of God." (1 Peter 4:10) God has designed us to be able to give to one another, in a special function. Just like the human body. Ears, eyes, heart, lungs, or liver-all have a different purpose, but work beautifully together to sustain the body.

"There are diversities of gifts, but the same Spirit. There are differences of ministries, but the same Lord. And there are diversities of activities, but it is the same God who works all in all." (1 Corinthians 12:4-6) We may have different gifts, but they all came from one God, and He has put them together to work in tandem with each other.

"Having then gifts differing according to the grace that is given to us, let us use them..." (Romans 12:6a) We are exhorted to use our gifts, and not hide them under a bushel.

"And to one he gave five talents, to another two, and to another one, to each according to his own ability" (Matthew 25:15a) This begins the passage of the parable of the ten talents. Like each man in this story, we are all given the appropriate gifts and responsibilities.

I need to point out something here. We all have a role to play in the furthering of the kingdom of God. Some are asked to do what people may see as a great thing. For example, speaking in a stadium of 50,000 people. God has gifted many men to do such a thing. Billy Graham comes to mind. But there so many smaller things that go into that event behind the scenes that we can be a part of. Or he may gift a man to speak in a pastoral role every Sunday, leading his flock.

But often, the gifts we are given can be used on a day-to-day basis and consist of some of the smallest details. For example, saying a kind word to someone. Picking up someone else's trash they left lying around. Sharing words of encouragement, giving a hug, being a prayer warrior. The list goes on and on.

"Then the righteous will answer Him, saying, 'Lord, when did we see You hungry and feed You, or thirsty and give You drink? When did we see You a stranger and take You in, or naked and clothe You? Or when did we see You sick, or in prison, and come to You?' And the King will answer and say to them, 'Assuredly, I say to you, inasmuch as you did it to one of the least of these My brethren, you did it to Me.'" (Matthew 25:37-40) Whatever kindness or Christlike behavior we exhibit, we need to remember that we are doing it unto the Lord. The passage also gives the flip side of that (verses 41-46).

"And whatever you do, do it heartily, as unto the Lord and not to men, knowing that from the Lord you will receive the reward of the inheritance; for you serve the Lord Christ." (Colossians 3:23-24) It doesn't matter what it is that God asks us to do, no matter how insignificant it may appear. To God it is a big thing. And He will reward us for our faithfulness. We are also told to do it to please God, not man.

To sum this all up, we will each be like one of the bean plants somewhere along the way. At times we feel totally rootbound, unable to spread our wings, so to speak. Other times we will be going along but end up dealing with some adversity along the way. And then there are those "mountaintop" experiences where we are thriving and producing fruit beyond our wildest expectations.

But whatever our situation is at the time, we need to remember that God can and will use us for His glory, if we have willing hearts.

There is something else we can learn from these beans. When it comes to being used by God, age doesn't matter. There is nobody too old or too young to be the hands and feet of Jesus. He has a plan and a purpose for every one of us. To be a part of God's kingdom-how exciting is that!!

REFLECTION TIME

Take a moment and examine how God has been using you lately. Which bean plant can you relate to the most and why?

_____

_____

_____

_____

Think of a time when God asked you to do something that seemed menial or unusual. What was your response?

_____

_____

_____

_____

How has God blessed you when you were obedient to His direction?

_____

_____

_____

_____

God has given you special gifts and talents. If you are not sure what they are, ask God to reveal them to you. Write out your prayer below.

_____

_____

_____

_____

Dear Heavenly Father:

Thank you for the privilege of serving in Your kingdom. It is beyond our comprehension that You, who is all powerful, would ask us to serve Your people. Please, through the power of the Holy Spirit, reveal to us what You are calling us to do, in any given situation. Thank You that we can be partakers of Your goodness. In Your precious name, Amen!

CALL TO ACTION!

Marching orders:

Ask the Lord to reveal to you some spiritual gifts He has given you. Write them in your journal, then decide to put them into practice. Trust me, you have gifts for the kingdom!

Ready, set, go!

OH, THAT WAGGING TONGUE

(The Power of Our Words)

SPEECH IS A WONDERFUL GIFT that God has given man. Many great speeches have been given throughout history. Powerful words have been uttered from the lips of people like John F Kennedy, Winston Churchill, Martin Luther King. Words that lift us up, encourage us, and inspire us. Of course, the most powerful words ever spoken came from the lips of our Lord and Savior, Jesus Christ, as He hung on the cross:

"IT IS FINISHED!" (John 19:30). Our relationship with Jesus was changed forevermore after that sentence was completed.

I think you would agree that very few people have that kind of impact on the world. But we do have an impact on those we encounter daily. Our words can be used to lift one another up. Sadly, they also can be used to tear people down. Far too often in that case, I hate to say. Gossip and lies spread like wildfire, if they are given their head.

Here is a little exercise for you. Think back to your childhood. Pick out a moment when someone said something that impacted your life for good. A teacher, a mentor, friend, sibling, or parent. Next, think of something that hurt, embarrassed, or deflated you. I would be willing to bet that the negative comment was easier to come up with than the positive one. Do you find yourself replaying memories from twenty, thirty years ago over something that really wasn't important, but it stuck with you?

Here is a simple, silly little thing that came to my mind while writing this, and it's for illustration purposes only. When I was in junior high school, I remember one morning walking past two boys. I heard one call out to me, "Hey high-waters!" (An expression used back then for pants that were too short at the ankles.) I was self-conscious about it the rest of the day, and those two words stuck with me, even though, as soon as the boy said them, he forgot about it. Now, forty- plus years later, when I try on a pair of pants, if the legs are too short, I think of the words "high water"! I need to point out that I am not traumatized by it, and lest you think I have led an extremely sheltered life and this is the worst I could come up with, there have been more hurtful things said to me than that. My point is, even the smallest "joke" can carry a punch.

Have you ever had an argument with someone, and years later, out of the blue, it comes to your mind? You rehash the entire scene, feeling the same emotions as if it just happened yesterday? Don't we hold onto the hurts that were long forgotten by the other person? I also think we need to be careful how we tease or criticize someone. It may seem like an innocent comment to you, but you never know that might have touched a hurt that was inflicted years ago. They may have heard a lifetime of "you're stupid, you can't do anything right," etc. One expression that I hate hearing is when somebody makes a cutting remark, then tacks on the end to soften it, "just kidding"! No, they weren't! There was some meaning behind the comment. There was a commercial that came out years ago, referring to verbal abuse. The description was, "words that hit like a fist." Physical bruises will heal, but emotional scars take a whole lot longer.

Jesus warns us about the power of the tongue, and our speech. It can be used to edify or to tear down.

"There is one who speaks like the piercings of a sword, but the tongue of the wise promotes health." (Proverbs 12:18) Thoughtless or casual comments feel like a knife going into the soul.

"Let no corrupt word proceed out of your mouth, but what is good for necessary edification, that it may impart grace to the hearers." (Ephesians 4:29) Uplifting speech can encourage one to great things.

"Whoever guards his mouth and tongue keeps his soul from troubles." (Proverbs 21:23) A piece of advice here: What *isn't* said cannot be repeated!

Alright, we have discussed the dangers of the tongue. How do we go about bridling it?

"A good man out of the good treasure of his heart brings forth good; and an evil man out of the evil treasure of his heart brings forth evil. For out of the abundance of the heart his mouth speaks." (Luke 6:45). Our words may come out of our mouths, but they originate within the depths of our heart and soul. Many deep-rooted thoughts come out in the heat of the moment that we would never say otherwise.

"Let the words of my mouth and the meditation of my heart be acceptable in Your sight, O Lord, my strength and my Redeemer." (Psalm 19:14) How do we know what words are pleasing to God? Study the very words He has given to us in the Bible. Check out this next verse:

"Finally, brethren, whatever things are true, whatever things are noble, whatever things are just, whatever things are pure, whatever things are lovely, whatever things are of good report, if there is any virtue and if there is anything praiseworthy—meditate on these things." (Philippians 4:8) This passage could be titled, Edifying Speech 101!

"But I say to you that for every idle word men may speak; they will give account of it in the day of judgment." (Matthew 12:36) Oh, my! Did anyone's heart just do a flip-flop? Is your mind racing over every word you have said?? If that isn't motivation to clean up our acts, well I don't know what is!

A good guideline to what is proper to say to someone is this acrostic:

T= Is it true?
H= Is it helpful?
I = Is it inspiring?
N= Is it necessary?
K= Is it kind?

If this is your mantra, your speech will be more fruitful and edifying. Of course, there are always those words that slip out in the moment. But if you are really striving to be in step with the words of God, then the heart is healthier, and those thoughts won't have taken root in the first place.

"Pleasant words are like a honeycomb, sweetness to the soul and health to the bones." (Proverbs 16:24) Amen!

REFLECTION TIME

Think of a time in your childhood when you were hurt, and a time when you were praised. Discuss the impact each of these had on you throughout your life.

_____

_____

_____

Now reverse the exercise. Think of something you said that hurt someone. Where was the source of those words, and how would you handle the situation in a Christ-like manner?

_____

_____

_____

Look at Luke 6:45 again. What are the good and bad treasures that may be rooted in your heart? How, using Philippians 4:8 as your guideline, can you increase the good, and get rid of the bad treasures?

_____

_____

_____

Using Psalm 19:14 as your motivation, write out a prayer asking God to show you what is acceptable to Him regarding your heart and speech, and to help you to weed out the gunk that has taken hold.

_____

_____

_____

Dear Father in Heaven:

Thank You for the gift of speech that differentiates us from your other created beings. Many great things have been accomplished through this gift. But sadly, like everything else, man continues to abuse the privilege. Forgive us for the idle talk, the hurtful words, the gossip and slander that fly around us constantly. They all stem from a wicked heart. You said in Your Word that the heart is deceitfully wicked. Help us to use our words to show love, kindness, encouragement. Help us to build up others, not to tear them down. We want our words and our thoughts to be pleasing to You, a sweet aroma. In Your strong name, Amen!

CALL TO ACTION!

Marching orders:

Go back to Philippian 4:8. Write in your journal each description of edifying speech. Then think of something you said recently that may have fallen short. What would have been a better approach? Is there someone you may have hurt with your speech? Ask the Lord to reveal it to you, and if you have the opportunity, step out and seek forgiveness. This isn't an easy challenge, but it can be very healing.

Ready, set, go!

DON'T GIVE UP
(The Christian Marathon)

HAVE YOU EVER FELT THAT you are stuck on a treadmill, walking and walking forever, but getting nowhere? It seems no matter how hard you work, you just can't see any progress. Weeding my garden often feels like that. It seems like for every weed I pull up, two more spring up in its place. Or paying bills. You get the month's bills all taken care of, and you think you can breathe for a moment. Then suddenly, the new month starts and the whole process begins again. Stuck in a never-ending cycle. You just can't seem to get ahead.

Life seems to be a series of these events. And there are times when we just want to give up; weary from the battle, drained of resources, and just plain done with it. I must wonder though, how often we are just one more stride away from victory. One more prayer that will break down that prison wall. Just one more mile until we reach the Promised Land. The idea of total victory has been replaced with the contentment of "good enough is good enough". How often do we fall short of God's full blessings in our lives?

Marathon runners often speak of "the wall". That dreaded point when your body has run out of energy before you run out of miles. Your resources have been drained, and you feel like you can't go on any farther. It's been described as somebody taking the plug out. It has brought an early end to many a runner's race.

The Christian walk can feel like that sometimes as well. You have prayed and prayed and prayed for deliverance, for healing, for a loved one's salvation. You are faithful, but you don't see anything happening. Weariness and discouragement set in. You have hit the wall. So how do we combat this?

God has addressed this issue quite nicely. Here are some choice passages for your consideration:

"In the day when I cried out, You answered me, and made me bold with strength in my soul." (Psalm 138:3) He hears us in our weakness, and will give us the strength we need for the task at hand.

"The Lord God is my strength; He will make my feet like deer's feet, and He will make me walk on my high hills." (Habakkuk 3:19) Deer have hooves that are made to climb over rocks and crevices. They can traverse swiftly and securely. God will give us what we need for the journey. Notice the passage said "high hills" not "high heels". Heels are not conducive for the arduous roads of the Christian walk. We need traction, ladies! Spiritual sneakers.

"And let us not grow weary while doing good, for in due season we shall reap if we do not lose heart." (Galatians 6:9) Sometimes we are just a prayer away from victory. The bounty is just around the bend.

Although we may grow weary physically, we often grow weary in our spirit as well. The battle is long and hard. The temptation may arise to just kick back and let others do the fighting. But don't give in to the wiles of the enemy. He wants nothing more than for you to throw in the towel.

So how do we stay focused and committed? The psalmists were constantly wrestling with this. How will you sustain me Lord? Do you hear my cry? What am I to do? Have you abandoned me? I am sure we all have asked these questions one time or another.

"I will lift up my eyes to the hills—from whence comes my help? My help comes from the Lord, who made heaven and earth. He will not allow your foot

to be moved; He who keeps you will not slumber." (Psalm 121:1-3) God never falls asleep at the wheel. He is always watching over us.

"My flesh and my heart fail; but God is the strength of my heart and my portion forever." (Psalm 73:26) God is everything the Christian will ever need.

There is no doubt about it. The Christian walk is not for the fainthearted. If you truly want to make a difference in the world, you can't just sit back, be comfortable, and live in your own bubble, just happy to get into the gates of heaven. That is not a fulfilled Christian life. And God has something more rewarding for you. Sometimes the road is scary. Sometimes there is a steep price to pay. The trials can be almost unbearable. But if God is calling you to something, rest assured that He will sustain you physically, spiritually, and mentally. That's what He promises in His Word:

"Fear not, for I have redeemed you; I have called you by your name; You are Mine. When you pass through the waters, I will be with you; and through the rivers, they shall not overflow you. When you walk through the fire, you shall not be burned, nor shall the flame scorch you. For I am the Lord your God, the Holy One of Israel, your Savior..." (Isaiah 43:1b-3a) He promises to be with us through every circumstance, right there beside us!

"I will both lie down in peace, and sleep; for You alone, O Lord, make me dwell in safety." (Psalm 4:8) We can sleep with both eyes shut! He will keep us safe.

Just a reminder-we aren't meant to be solo Christians. We are all in this together, serving the same God, with the same mission. To know Him and make Him known. Paul exhorts us *"Rejoice with those who rejoice, and weep with those who weep".* (Romans 12:15) and to *"bear one another's burdens, and so fulfill the law of Christ.".* (Galatians 6:2)

When the Israelites were fighting Amalek, as long as Moses kept his arms raised, they were victorious. When he became fatigued, Aaron and Hur came alongside him and held his arms up. Victory was achieved. Read the full story in Exodus 17.

So, are you fighting the good fight? Are you seeking the Lord for your strength? Are you Moses, getting weary and needing the assistance of your Christian brother or sister? If so, look up to Jesus, then look out to others. You will be victorious and reap the harvest God has for you.

REFLECTION TIME

Are there times when you are just plain weary from fighting the spiritual battle? Think of a recent trial. How did God sustain you through it?

_____

_____

_____

_____

Think of a deer scaling a mountainside, so surefooted. How does the passage of Habakkuk 3:19 give you comfort in your personal walk?

_____

_____

_____

_____

Choose one of the scriptures from today's devotional that ministered to your heart. Commit it to memory. Why did this one speak to you?

_____

_____

_____

_____

Write out a prayer asking God to strengthen and sustain you through your personal journey with Him. Ask Him to show you how to achieve that peace and comfort needed.

_____

_____

_____

_____

Heavenly Father:

Thank you that You supply all of our needs for this crazy Christian life. You told us it would not be an easy journey. But we thank You that we do not have to walk it alone. We can call out to You in any moment, and trust that You will hear our cries. Thank you for the strong Christian brothers and sisters you put across our paths, so we can love and encourage one another. Help us not to be stealth Christians, just flying under the radar. This walk can be bold, exciting and so rewarding if we just step out in faith and trust You. Be our guide, and let us hear Your voice so we don't go off track. Give us the strength to finish our race, so we can hear those beautiful words, "Well done, good and faithful servant. Enter into the joy of your Lord." In Your Name we pray, Amen!

CALL TO ACTION!

Marching orders:

Take an honest look at your Christian walk. Are you finding yourself kicking back, just cruising along in stealth mode? Reflect on ways that you can have a more active Christian life, how you can have a bigger impact on the kingdom. List five things that you can do. Write them in your journal.

Ready, set, go!

THE ELEVENTH HOUR

(Trusting God)

SOMETIMES THIS LIFE FEELS LIKE a scene in a disaster movie. The floodwaters are rising and time is running out. Will we make it to safety before we are overcome by the waves or will we drown before help comes to rescue us?

I am sure you can relate to the experience at some time in your life where you felt your back was against the wall, or maybe the calendar. You have 30 days until this, or a week until that, and you don't see a way out of the predicament.

A couple of years ago, when we rented a house in another town, the owner decided that he was going to sell the house and we needed to move. It's very hard to find rental property when you have pets. We searched and searched but to no avail. When the house finally sold, we had 30 days. We prayed and hunted. A few things looked promising, but for some reason or other, they fell through. It was ten days before Christmas, and escrow closed on the 19th. We had many people praying for us. Finally, on December 16, we found a place! We moved that weekend, and on Monday, we had the final walk through with the property manager. Whew! A white-knuckle ride, but God was faithful to provide at the eleventh hour. He likes to do that...

I am reminded of a couple of Bible stories where God intervened at the brink of disaster. Abraham's sacrifice comes to mind. The story is found in Genesis 22. God directs Abraham to sacrifice his son Isaac on the altar. Just as he is ready to plunge the knife into his son, God stops him. It was a test of Abraham's faith and he passed with flying colors.

Another story is the fiery furnace talked about in Daniel 3. King Nebuchadnezzar ordered Shadrach, Meshach, and Abed-Nego to be burned alive in the fiery furnace because they refused to bow down and worship him. Even though they faced certain death, they trusted God to spare them. And at the eleventh hour, He did just that.

We may deduce from these scriptures, and our personal experiences that God is indeed the God of the eleventh hour, just waiting until we are losing our grip and then He decides to get involved and swoops down and rescues us. But that is not Biblical. He doesn't just sit back and wait until we are at the end of our rope to act. He is there the entire time; His hand is fully on the situation. He knows exactly what He is doing, and when and why He will do it.

The men in these two Bible stories were able to demonstrate their faith in God because they knew their Lord. They trusted and believed that God was faithful. But there are scriptures where the writer did cry out in despair, feeling that God was not hearing them.

Sometimes we may think He is too late. Mary and Martha experienced that very thing when their brother Lazarus died. Jesus delayed His coming when He heard Lazarus was sick. By the time Jesus arrived, Lazarus had passed. But Jesus had a plan. This was His response upon being summoned: *"When Jesus heard that, He said, 'This sickness is not unto death, but for the glory of God, that the Son of God may be glorified through it.'"* (John 11:4) But Jesus was doing a work in the heart of the sisters and glorifying His Father.

"But, beloved, do not forget this one thing, that with the Lord one day is as a thousand years, and a thousand years as one day. The Lord is not slack concerning His promise, as some count slackness, but is longsuffering toward us, not willing that any should perish but that all should come to repentance."

(2 Peter 3:8-9) Sometimes we question God's delay in answering our prayers. But He has a perfect plan with perfect timing. He is never late.

"The Lord your God in your midst, the Mighty One, will save; He will rejoice over you with gladness, He will quiet you with His love, He will rejoice over you with singing." (Zephaniah 3:17) Israel was praising God for His deliverance. He promises to deliver us as well.

"For I am persuaded that neither death nor life, nor angels nor principalities nor powers, nor things present nor things to come, nor height nor depth, nor any other created thing, shall be able to separate us from the love of God which is in Christ Jesus our Lord." (Romans 8:38-39) Though sometimes we may feel a separation from God, the truth is that there is nothing that CAN separate us from His love, no matter the situation.

"Yea, though I walk through the valley of the shadow of death, I will fear no evil; for You are with me; Your rod and Your staff, they comfort me." (Psalm 23:4) We can take comfort in knowing that God is with us, no matter the circumstance.

As we grow deeper in our walk with Jesus, we will come to learn that God is always with us, He has His hand on our situation. He is not worried about the outcome; so we should not be. If we are doing our due diligence, that is praying earnestly, trusting Him, doing the practical things that need to be done (like house hunting in my experience) then we can trust that it will work out.

The gospels speak of the time when Jesus and the disciples were in a boat on the sea of Galilee and a fierce storm came up. Jesus was fast asleep. But the guys, some who were seasoned fishermen, were terrified that they were going to drown. But after Jesus woke up, He calmed the sea with just a word. They were astonished! Jesus had this question for them: *"But He said to them, 'Where is your faith?' And they were afraid, and marveled, saying to one another, 'Who can this be? For He commands even the winds and water, and they obey Him!'"* (Luke 8:25). Who indeed! Just the Creator of the universe, is all…

We need to also remember that God may be working in our situation to reveal Himself to someone else. In other words, it's not always about us! But no matter the reason for the late hour, it is a far better thing than if He had rushed in and fixed it immediately. When you know in your heart of hearts that God did the impossible, the victory is so much sweeter!

REFLECTION TIME

Think of a time when you felt your back was against the wall. How did God intervene and deliver you?

_____

_____

_____

_____

There are many psalms where the writer is crying out in despair, thinking that God has abandoned him. But by the end of the psalm, the writer was giving praise to God. Have you experienced that feeling that God has abandoned you?

_____

_____

_____

_____

Choose one of the stories we discussed, or one of the scriptures. How does it speak to your heart?

_____

_____

_____

_____

Write out a prayer thanking God for His faithfulness, and to help you to trust that He will work in whatever situation you are facing.

_____

_____

_____

Dear Heavenly Father:

Thank you that we can rest and trust in You that You will always have our back. We know that You love us and want good things for us. Help us to always remember that You have a purpose for everything that You do, and that when we come out on the other side of the trial, we will be stronger, and closer to You for having gone through it. But just as importantly, help us to remember these things while we are in the midst of the trial, because we know that You are always there IN the storm. Thank you. In Your strong name, Amen!

CALL TO ACTION!

Marching orders:

Reflect on how you respond when you are in the "eleventh hour". Using the scripture passages, how would you minister to someone who is in that situation. Reach out to that person and minster to them.

Ready, set, go!

HOW DO I LOVE THEE?

(Seeking a Deep Love for Jesus)

TODAY IS DAY FOURTEEN, AND the topic is about love. I imagine right now you are having visions of valentine hearts, candy, and roses. But this is being written on November 14, and the only vision I have dancing around in my head right now is turkey and pumpkin pie in two weeks!

So why the topic on love? Well, a dear sister in Christ mentioned to me of having a profound love for Jesus. In her personal studies, she has found that although she loves Jesus, she doesn't feel that profound, deep love for Him that she thought she had. She asked me, "How does one have that love?" It's not an easy question to answer. But since it is a Biblical topic, I thought we would explore what the Bible says about love.

There are four types of love discussed in the Bible. The one we are interested in is "Agape" love. This love is of and from God, whose very nature is love itself.

A common mistake people make regarding love is that it is a feeling, and that is how we gauge our relationships. It is something we fall in and out of, depending on the circumstances. Love as an emotion is selfish. It's based on self. How do I feel? What do I get from this relationship? But it is far more than that; it is an action. It is something that we do. It is the action of giving of self, without expecting something in return. It is putting the welfare of others before us, caring for others even though they may be our enemies.

God is the epitome of this kind of love. Everything He does is out of this unconditional and profound love that He has for us. Even when we have been so unlovable!

"But God demonstrates His own love toward us, in that while we were still sinners, Christ died for us." (Romans 5:8) The cross was the most sacrificial love that could be given.

"But God, who is rich in mercy, because of His great love with which He loved us, even when we were dead in trespasses, made us alive together with Christ (by grace you have been saved), and raised us up together, and made us sit together in the heavenly places in Christ Jesus, that in the ages to come He might show the exceeding riches of His grace in His kindness toward us in Christ Jesus." (Ephesians 2:4-7)

In John 21:15-17, after Jesus has been resurrected, He is sitting on the shore with Peter. He asked Peter three times "Do you love me?" Jesus used the agape word for love. The first two times Peter answered yes, he used the "phileo" form of love (brotherly love). It was the third time around that Jesus used the phileo word, and again Peter responded in kind. There are many differing opinions about what this means. Is it conceivable that God recognizes it is almost impossible for us feeble human beings to love with that totally unconditional love that Jesus gives us? To give all that we have, to sacrifice everything for Jesus? To love as He loves? This can only be done through the Holy Spirit that resides in us.

In Revelation, Chapter 2, Jesus rebuked the church of Ephesus for having left their first love. Although they did all the right things- their works, labor and patient endurance-their fire had died out. Their joy and passion had faded. That can happen. The newness fades away. Life sets in, we get busy, neglect spending time with Jesus. Or we get so busy serving in the name of Jesus, that we neglect the very One we are serving. Can we get so distracted just doing life that we take our relationship with Him for granted, and then realize we have drifted a bit? I am not talking about walking away from Jesus. I am talking about neglecting Him.

So how do we get back to loving Jesus, or discover that love on a deeper level? I am not interested in a "7 steps to a better relationship" approach. But I can suggest a few things that will help in drawing closer to Jesus, and thus deepen our love for Him. To know Him is to love Him. Our entire Christian life flows from that knowledge. So here goes:

Pray to Him. Talk to God. Tell Him what you are thinking. He already knows, so you won't hurt His feelings. By openly acknowledging your problem, you open the door for Him to help you. Set aside a time for regular prayer. Communication is vital to any healthy relationship. *"The effective, fervent prayer of a righteous man avails much."* (James 5:16)

Praise Him. Sit down with a notebook or journal, and list all the attributes of God. Meditate on His goodness. Do some research on the names of God. Spend time just thanking Him for everything around you. *"I will praise You, O Lord my God, with all my heart, and I will glorify Your name forevermore."* (Psalm 86:12)

Study the Word. Choose a book of the Bible and read it. But not just on the surface. Dig into it. Study it. Find a commentary on it and go verse by verse. There are great commentary resources online. *"Your words were found, and I ate them, and Your Word was to me the joy and rejoicing of my heart; for I am called by Your name, O Lord God of hosts."* (Jeremiah 15:16)

Attend a regular Bible study. It is so important to have a regular schedule of studying God's Word, learning from men whom God has gifted to teach His Word. Find a church that teaches from the Bible and commit to attending regularly. If you cannot physically attend a church, find a teaching online or on the radio and commit to watching/listening to it on a regular basis. There are many awesome Bible teachers. Research what the doctrines of their church are. Be careful of "fluff" and "itchy ear" stuff. It is best to find one that teaches through a full book of the Bible. Set aside a specific time each week. Make Sunday study a priority. Add Wednesday nights, for extra measure! **And turn off all the distractions!**

Fellowship with others. We are a body of believers, designed to work together, to encourage and love one another. *"As iron sharpens iron, so a man sharpens the countenance of his friend."* (Proverbs 27:17)

Ok, I gave you five. But the most important thing to remember is to seek Him, learn of Him, press into Him. Don't let the cares, interests, and busyness of this world undermine your relationship with Him. Make Him the number one priority in your life and rededicate yourself to this relationship.

I would be remiss if I didn't address a key area of drawing closer to Jesus, which would be number six on the list. That is through the trials of this world. We cannot waste the important lessons that God wants to teach us through them. There is no better way to become closer to Him than to cling to Him as a child clings to his earthly father. Use this time of suffering to call out to Him, asking Him for His protection, provision, peace, comfort, whatever it is you need. He will wrap His loving arms around you. I would say, that's intimate!

"Draw near to God and He will draw near to you." (James 4:8) That's a promise!

REFLECTION TIME

Are you feeling that there is a closeness lacking in your relationship with Jesus? How would you describe it?

_____

_____

_____

_____

Reflect on your daily schedule. Are there things that you have allowed to get in the way of your time with Jesus? What has taken priority over Him?

_____

_____

_____

_____

Look at the suggestions to help you draw closer to Jesus. Choose one or two to focus on over the next month. How will you implement them?

_____

_____

_____

_____

Write out a prayer, asking God to help you honor your commitment to draw closer to Him.

_____

_____

_____

_____

Dear Heavenly Father:

We are so thankful that you have a loving and forgiving heart. You understand our human frailties. And it doesn't matter how far we drift, or what we have done. You are always ready to forgive and restore us. Please help us to ignite that fire that we once had. To return to our first love, You, and be a burning flame for your kingdom. We love you and we praise you! In Your precious name, Amen!

CALL TO ACTION!

Marching orders:

Expand your thoughts on question #3. Come up with a specific action plan to implement them and write them in your journal. Then start putting them into practice!

Ready, set, go!

WHAT A TANGLED WEB WE WEAVE

(The Art of Deception)

WOULDN'T IT BE WONDERFUL IF people always told the truth, if their motives were pure, and we could always trust each other? Imagine an honest politician! I know, I am living in a fantasy world. Lying and deception have been around since the Garden of Eden, when Satan duped Eve into thinking she could disobey God. And we have been paying the price ever since.

Deception rears its ugly head in many different forms. First, there are flat-out lies; the lies of commission. Then, there are the lies of omission, where we didn't exactly lie, but we left out a few things or failed to correct a misconception in order to hide the truth.

Have you ever told a "little white lie" to supposedly spare someone's feelings? Or how about that social fib to get out of an invitation. We tend to rationalize these things, but we know that lying is still lying.

Deception has many other forms as well. Cheating on your taxes or an expense report, infidelity, lying to your parents about where you have been, overcharging clients on jobs. The list goes on and on. We have all been guilty of lying at one time or another. Sadly, some people seem to make a career of it, and are masters at it. Here are some Biblical stories of deception:

"Jacob said to his father, 'I am Esau your firstborn; I have done just as you told me; please arise, sit and eat of my game, that your soul may bless me.'" (Genesis 27:19) Jacob, with the help of his mother, cheated his brother Esau out of his birthright.

"Now Abraham said of Sarah his wife, 'She is my sister.' And Abimelech king of Gerar sent and took Sarah." (Genesis 20:2) This was the first of two times that Abraham tried to pass Sarah off as his sister.

"So it came to pass in the morning, that behold, it was Leah. And he said to Laban, 'What is this you have done to me? Was it not for Rachel that I served you? Why then have you deceived me?'" (Genesis 29:25) Laban deceived Jacob by passing Leah off as Rachel and Jacob ended up marrying the wrong gal.

Then there's the story of Joseph being sold by his brothers, and they told their father that he was dead. (Genesis 37)

Whoa! All this deception, and we are still in Genesis! We have an adversary who is the master deceiver. Satan has been lying and manipulating, deceiving, taunting for centuries, and he has become very, very good at it. He has caused more destruction in this world than all the wars put together.

"He who sins is of the devil, for the devil has sinned from the beginning. For this purpose the Son of God was manifested, that He might destroy the works of the devil." (1 John 3:8) One day, Satan will be permanently put out of commission!

"You are of your father the devil, and the desires of your father you want to do. He was a murderer from the beginning, and does not stand in the truth, because there is no truth in him. When he speaks a lie, he speaks from his own resources, for he is a liar and the father of it." (John 8:44)

Satan's sole purpose is to steal, kill, and destroy.

Deception in the church is another huge issue that we are warned about in the Bible. There are men and women, who proclaim to know God's Word, but use their lies to distort it. It can be very subtle.

"Beware of false prophets, who come to you in sheep's clothing, but inwardly they are ravenous wolves. You will know them by their fruits." (Matthew 7:15-16). These false prophets appear and then speak like they are true ambassadors of God's Word. Like Satan, they will lure you in, very subtly, and you may not even realize that they are distorting the truth.

"For when they speak great swelling words of emptiness, they allure through the lusts of the flesh, through lewdness, the ones who have actually escaped from those who live in error. While they promise them liberty, they themselves are slaves of corruption; for by whom a person is overcome, by him also he is brought into bondage." (2 Peter 2:18-19)

These false teachers lure people with grandiose speech, but really saying nothing of value. But the people are lured into the snare, like a spider lures its prey into its web.

"Nevertheless, I have a few things against you, because you allow that woman Jezebel, who calls herself a prophetess, to teach and seduce My servants to commit sexual immorality and eat things sacrificed to idols. And I gave her time to repent of her sexual immorality, and she did not repent." (Revelation 2:20-21) Here Jesus is rebuking the church of Thyatira for allowing the false doctrine to enter the church. There will be great repercussions for tolerating and even embracing this false doctrine.

With so much deception coming at us from the pulpit, the radio, television, books, how do we guard ourselves from the lies?

"These were more fair-minded than those in Thessalonica, in that they received the word with all readiness, and searched the Scriptures daily to find out whether these things were so." (Acts 17:11) The Bereans made a practice

to examine the words being spoken to those in the Word. Always compare everything against scripture.

"Be diligent to present yourself approved to God, a worker who does not need to be ashamed, rightly dividing the word of truth." (2 Timothy 2:15) We must never mismanage or misuse the Word of God. False teachers will twist the word in any direction that suits their purpose.

"Beware lest anyone cheat you through philosophy and empty deceit, according to the tradition of men, according to the basic principles of the world, and not according to Christ." (Colossians 2:8) Immerse yourself in the Word of God, so the deceiver cannot rip you off!

REFLECTION TIME

Think of a time when you were deceived. What were the tactics of the enemy in the situation?

_____

_____

_____

_____

How can you use the Word of God to counteract deception?

_____

_____

_____

_____

Study Acts 17:11. How can you be more like the Bereans in discerning the truth of what you hear compared to the Bible?

_____

_____

_____

_____

Write out a prayer asking God to help you to recognize the subtle devices of the enemy, and to stand in the truth of His Word.

_____

_____

_____

_____

_____

Dear Heavenly Father:

We are in a constant battle with the enemy and all his deceitful tactics. Sometimes they come in the form of false teachers, even through people we know and love. Help us to remember that the enemy is relentless and he will look for that button he can push with us. Help us to recognize the lies, and to know Your Word so well that we can see the lie immediately. Thank You for the Holy Spirit who resides in us to guide and protect us. We never want to go astray from the truth. Help us to hold it close to our hearts. In Your Precious Name, Amen!

CALL TO ACTION!

Marching orders:

Read the account of Joseph and his brothers in Genesis 37. Think about how he handled all the adversity. Apply that to a difficult situation you may be facing or have recently been through. What is your plan of action using Joseph as your role model?

Ready, set, go!

HITTING THE SNOOZE BUTTON
(I Will Get Around to Jesus!)

I HAVE NEVER UNDERSTOOD THE snooze button theory. I guess the idea is that it allows you to catch a few extra z's before you drag yourself out of bed. An extra ten minutes of sleep. Some people hit it more than once. But my preference is to snooze through until the alarm rings, then get up. I don't want my sleep interrupted any more than it already is through the night!

Some people go through life with a perpetual snooze button attitude. Just let me have a little more time before I do this or start that. Procrastination is a way of life for them. I don't mean to throw stones, for goodness knows I have done this a lot in my life. I didn't come to receive the Lord until I was 42!

I have discovered as I have grown older, that putting things off doesn't make them go away. It seems that the pile gets bigger and bigger. It is much more conducive to peace of mind to simply take care of business as it comes up and get it off the agenda. Otherwise my mind is constantly being nagged by my conscience that there is something waiting to be done.

There are many phrases that people have taken on as their mantra. "Don't do today what you can put off until tomorrow." How about that famous line from *Gone With the Wind*- "I'll think about it tomorrow"? Oh, and *Annie* with the little redheaded girl singing about how tomorrow is always a day away… (sorry, I didn't mean to put that tune in your head).

But, like most everything we humans do or think, the Bible seems to take a different approach. And God doesn't let us down here either:

"The soul of a lazy man desires, and has nothing; but the soul of the diligent shall be made rich." (Proverbs 13:4) Laziness does nothing to accomplish the deed at hand. But the hard worker will be successful.

"The sluggard does not plow in the autumn; he will seek at harvest and have nothing." (Proverbs 20:4) Without the plowing, there will be no planting, and then later, no harvest. Procrastination leads to empty baskets.

"Do not boast about tomorrow, for you do not know what a day may bring forth." (Proverbs 27:1) It is better to take care of things today, for you do not know what tomorrow will bring to you. I love the book of Proverbs, don't you? Right to the point on just about any topic.

Jesus spoke of a more pressing matter of taking care of business. He was concerned with eternal matters:

"Let your waist be girded and your lamps burning; and you yourselves be like men who wait for their master, when he will return from the wedding, that when he comes and knocks, they may open to him immediately. Blessed are those servants whom the master, when he comes, will find watching." (Luke 12:35-37a) We need to be in constant expectancy for His return.

"Therefore, you also be ready, for the Son of Man is coming at an hour you do not expect." (Luke 12:40) Jesus is summing up what He stated in the previous scripture. We need to be ready and watchful. Not slacking in our diligence.

"The Lord is not slack concerning His promise, as some count slackness, but is longsuffering toward us, not willing that any should perish but that all should come to repentance." (2 Peter 3:9) People have been waiting a long time for Jesus to call us to heaven. But He is not procrastinating; He is waiting for more to come to Him. But there will be a day when His waiting is over. I pray we will all be ready.

"In an acceptable time, I have heard you, and in the day of salvation I have helped you. Behold, now is the accepted time; behold, now is the day of salvation." (2 Corinthians 6:2) Paul is speaking to unbelievers, exhorting them to make the decision to follow Jesus. Notice that he said today. Not tomorrow, not when I feel like it. Why? Because folks, tomorrow is promised to no one, despite what Scarlett O'Hara and Annie might proclaim!

So, as you can see, procrastination can take on many different forms. From paying that bill, to addressing our very eternal destiny. From my vantage point now, I find it amazing that people cannot see how vitally important it is to have a right relationship with Jesus. But then I remember that I can take to heart what the blind man said after Jesus restored his sight. *"One thing I know: that though I was blind, now I see."* (John 9:25) This is a great story about how the blind man was healed and the Pharisees were livid with his answers. (We will dissect this story in Book 3). But suffice it to say, that before we came to receive Jesus, we were all blind. But by taking off the scales, we can see clearly.

Each one of us has an appointed time for our earthly life to end. There is a sense of urgency in the Bible about not delaying that crucial decision. Because once you take your final breath here on earth, your eternal destiny has been decided. There are no do-overs. Tomorrow is promised to no one, and I guarantee you that each soul in heaven is not feeling a single moment of regret for having made the right decision. The rapture of the church may not come for another hundred years. But we each will face our own personal "rapture". The last thing I want to hear is Jesus saying to me, "depart from Me I never knew you."

Don't hit the snooze button on your life. Get up, be about your Father's business. Embrace and rejoice in everything He has set before you. Because there's no place for thoughts of "what might have been" in the Christian walk. Amen?

REFLECTION TIME

Have you been plagued with that "snooze button" mentality? Think of a time when you really put something off. Why was that, and how did you feel about it?

_____

_____

_____

_____

Reflecting on your previous answer, how does the scriptures change the way you approach things? What would you have done differently?

_____

_____

_____

_____

Choose one of the scriptures in today's devotional. Commit it to memory. How does this one speak to your heart?

_____

_____

_____

_____

Write out a prayer asking God to help you with any areas that you tend to put off, especially when it comes to spiritual matters.

_____

_____

_____

_____

Dear Heavenly Father:

Sometimes we can be such sluggards. Doing what we want, and when we want to do them, postponing them until they go from molehills to mountains. But one thing we do not want to put off or ignore is our relationship with You, the author and finisher of our faith, the One who holds our very breath in His hands. Help us to have a sense of urgency, and a desire to do what You are calling us to do, and when You are calling us to do it, tear down our self-appointed timetables. Let our cry be, "Here I am Lord, send me". Thank you, Jesus! In Your name, Amen!

CALL TO ACTION!

Marching orders:

This is literally a call to action. No more procrastination! I want you to zero in on that one thing you keep putting off. I have a feeling a few thoughts popped into your mind. Ask the Lord to reveal the one He wants you to deal with, and how He wants you to attack it. Put His words into action and just take care of business. You will feel better when you are done. Honest!

Ready, set, go!

SLINGS AND ARROWS

(Forgiving One Another)

SOMEWHERE ALONG THE LINE, WE have all suffered from the pain inflicted upon us by others, whether it be a loved one, a coworker, or even a total stranger. It hurts. The wounds can go deep. The pain can be physical, emotional, or verbal. Wounds from betrayal, deceit, humiliation the list goes on.

Sadly, we can hold onto the hurts long after the other person is out of our lives. The perpetrator probably won't even remember the incident. But we relive the memories like it happened yesterday, even though it was years ago.

Some cling to these wounds like an anchor. But the anchor doesn't save us. Instead, it drags us down, grounding us in our muck and mire. It's like the albatross in the poem, a psychological burden that hinders us.

So, what is the answer here? I will give you an eleven-letter word that you aren't going to like. Forgiveness. Oh… I can just hear it now. "After what that bozo did to me? You expect me to forgive him?? Not on your life! Not even if he crawls across broken glass for twenty miles. Nope. Never. I won't forgive. Instead, I am going to make him pay for the rest of his life. (Snarl…)

Ok, maybe you aren't thinking that. And I don't mean to make light of a truly deep wound. But that doesn't change the fact that forgiveness is not only like a healing balm, it is Biblical.

"Therefore, as the elect of God, holy and beloved, put on tender mercies, kindness, humility, meekness, longsuffering; bearing with one another, and forgiving one another, if anyone has a complaint against another; even as Christ forgave you, so you also must do." (Colossians 3:12-13). Did you catch that last line, about Christ forgiving you? And that we **must** forgive. It's not a suggestion. It is a command.

"For if you forgive men their trespasses, your heavenly Father will also forgive you. But if you do not forgive men their trespasses, neither will your Father forgive your trespasses." (Matthew 6:14-15) Uh-oh. Certainly, we cannot expect God to forgive us when we are harboring unforgiveness in our heart toward others.

"Let all bitterness, wrath, anger, clamor, and evil speaking be put away from you, with all malice. And be kind to one another, tenderhearted, forgiving one another, even as God in Christ forgave you." (Ephesians 4:31-32) Unresolved anger turns into bitterness. And bitterness will eat away at our souls like a cancer.

"Then Peter came to Him and said, 'Lord, how often shall my brother sin against me, and I forgive him? Up to seven times?' Jesus said to him, 'I do not say to you, up to seven times, but up to seventy times seven.'" (Matthew 18:21-22). Jesus isn't referring to a literal 490 times. But He is saying that there are no bounds to forgiveness. Think about it. How many times have you gone to the Lord asking for forgiveness for the same sin?

"For to this you were called, because Christ also suffered for us, leaving us an example, that you should follow His steps: 'Who committed no sin, nor was deceit found in His mouth'; who, when He was reviled, did not revile in return; when He suffered, He did not threaten, but committed Himself to Him who judges righteously." (1 Peter 2:21-23) We cannot exact vengeance on those who have wronged us. That is up to the Lord to do so.

"Then Jesus said, 'Father, forgive them, for they do not know what they do.'" (Luke 23:34) How can we hold back forgiveness when Jesus was able to ask

for forgiveness for those who brutally beat Him and wrongly crucified Him? Can our pain measure up to that?

But what if this person is not repentant over what he or she has done? Or what if I forgive them and they continue to commit the wrong against me?

"But I say to you, love your enemies, bless those who curse you, do good to those who hate you, and pray for those who spitefully use you and persecute you." (Luke 6:27-28). Repaying evil with kindness can confuse and stop the vilest of behaviors. But it's a good idea, in my opinion, to stay out of the line of fire!

"Beloved, do not avenge yourselves, but rather give place to wrath; for it is written, 'Vengeance is Mine, I will repay,' says the Lord." (Romans 12:19) God will take care of them in due time.

There are some things we need to understand about forgiveness that might help us out. First and foremost, forgiveness is NOT absolution from consequences. Just as we ask for forgiveness, we still may have to pay the cost of the sinful act. I may be sorry I shot that person, but that doesn't mean I won't do jail time. So, we don't have to absolve the person who hurt us from making things right, if possible.

Nor is forgiveness a feeling. It is an action. It is not reasonable to believe that when you forgive someone your pain automatically disappears. But it should certainly help you work through it. I heard someone describe it like peeling an onion. Layer upon layer. But you need to take the first step.

When you hold onto the hurt, your hurt turns to anger, then anger turns to bitterness. And guess what? That puts you right in the middle of sin. Yes, bitterness is one of those things that defile us.

"Pursue peace with all people, and holiness, without which no one will see the Lord: looking carefully lest anyone fall short of the grace of God; lest any root

of bitterness springing up cause trouble, and by this many become defiled." (Hebrews 12:14-15)

So, examine your heart, and see if there is any unforgiveness, anger, or bitterness harboring in there against someone who has hurt you. Forgive as you have been forgiven, and free yourself of the burden of the pain. God will take care of things!

REFLECTION TIME

Think of a time when you have experienced being hurt by somebody. Is it resolved in your heart, or are you still holding onto it?

_____

_____

_____

_____

Reflect on the things that you have done that God has forgiven you for. How can you apply that same attitude to the situation above?

_____

_____

_____

_____

Choose one of the scriptures from today's devotional. Commit it to memory. How does it speak to you?

_____

_____

_____

_____

Write out a prayer asking God to help you forgive the person who has hurt you, and to help you let go of the pain.

_____

_____

_____

_____

Dear Heavenly Father:

Thank You that You love us with unconditional love. Thank you that You have made a way for us to be forgiven of every sin we have ever committed. Sometimes it is so hard to let go of the hurts that have been inflicted upon us. But Your Son gave us the ultimate example of forgiveness at the cross. Please help us to be able to forgive as Jesus did. We lift up those who have hurt us, we ask that You bless them, and that You do a mighty work in their hearts as well. In Your name, Amen!

CALL TO ACTION!

Marching orders:

Today's assignment may be a tough one. There are actually two calls today. Think of someone whom you have hurt or offended. Take it to the Lord. Then go to that person, either in person or, if not possible, make a phone call or write a letter asking for their forgiveness.

Secondly, think of someone who has hurt you. Taking the same action, seek the Lord, then go to that person and forgive them. Yes, and without rehashing the point or the episode. Just forgive. Forgiveness is very freeing. And it leads to healing.

Ready, set, go!

OH, THE GOOD OLD DAYS
(Don't Look Back)

AS WE GROW OLDER, WE tend to reminisce about days past. Somehow, the memories seem to grow sweeter as time marches on. Around the holidays I grow nostalgic about the family gatherings around the huge dinner table, favorite dishes, and family traditions. Or the first day of freedom at the end of the school year and looking forward to swimming in the pool and the annual camping vacations.

Sometimes in our trips down memory lane, we can whitewash the struggles, and put things in a better light than they should be. That can get us into trouble. There are things better left in the past. Maybe that friend we hung around with in high school that always got us into trouble, or sneaking out to places we had no business being in.

It can be a dangerous thing living in the past. Longing for the way things used to be. Especially when we are struggling a bit in the present, trying to adjust to changes. Maybe you have recently changed jobs. You're finding the new responsibilities challenging. You think back about that job you left, and question whether you made the right decision. "I was comfortable there. I knew what I was supposed to do, and I did it." But you have forgotten a few things. How about that hour commute in rush hour traffic? Or that coworker who gossiped about you, or how many times you left work drained and burned out, thinking how you hated your job?

There are a couple of stories in the Bible about people who longed for the past. The classic one is the Israelites as they were headed for the Promised Land. Granted, 40 years was probably a lot longer than anyone imagined it would take. But here is the scenario:

They had been enslaved in Egypt. Treated horribly by the guards, given food that was left over. Their opportunity for freedom came through Moses. But after years of wandering, they whined and complained.

"Now the mixed multitude who were among them yielded to intense craving; so the children of Israel also wept again and said: 'Who will give us meat to eat? We remember the fish which we ate freely in Egypt, the cucumbers, the melons, the leeks, the onions, and the garlic; but now our whole being is dried up; there is nothing at all except this manna before our eyes!'" (Numbers 11:4-6). To be honest, I can't imagine eating the same food day in and day out for every single meal. But what they are forgetting is the food they received in Egypt was the leftovers from the plates of their captors. The manna that was provided was a miracle from God. This was the Lord's response:

"Then you shall say to the people, 'Consecrate yourselves for tomorrow, and you shall eat meat; for you have wept in the hearing of the Lord, saying, 'Who will give us meat to eat? For it was well with us in Egypt'. Therefore, the Lord will give you meat, and you shall eat. You shall eat, not one day, nor two days, nor five days, nor ten days, nor twenty days, but for a whole month, until it comes out of your nostrils and becomes loathsome to you, because you have despised the Lord who is among you, and have wept before Him, saying, 'Why did we ever come up out of Egypt?'" (Numbers 11:18-20) Lesson here? Don't anger the Lord with whining and complaining! Oh, then He caused a plague to come upon them. I imagine while they were reeling from the plague, they started longing for the manna again.

Another story about looking back in longing is spoken of in Genesis. Lot and his family were hanging out in the gate of the wicked city of Sodom. Because of its depravity, God sought to destroy Sodom and Gomorrah. He sent angels to warn Lot to take his family and flee. Let's pick up the story here:

"When the morning dawned, the angels urged Lot to hurry, saying, 'Arise, take your wife and your two daughters who are here, lest you be consumed in the punishment of the city.' And while he lingered, the men took hold of his hand, his wife's hand, and the hands of his two daughters, the Lord being merciful to him, and they brought him out and set him outside the city. So it came to pass, when they had brought them outside, that he said, 'Escape for your life! Do not look behind you nor stay anywhere in the plain. Escape to the mountains, lest you be destroyed.'" (Genesis 19:15-17) The instructions were clear, but Lot's wife did not listen. *"But his wife looked back behind him, and she became a pillar of salt."* (Genesis 19:26) Even though Mrs. Lot physically left the evil city, her heart remained, and fell victim to God's judgment. Interestingly, Jesus referred to this in Luke 17:32, reminding us to remember her. He was warning us about the coming of His kingdom.

"And Jesus said to him, 'No one, having put his hand to the plow, and looking back, is fit for the kingdom of God.'" (Luke 9:62) Jesus isn't speaking of salvation here, but of being a productive servant.

"Brethren, I do not count myself to have apprehended; but one thing I do, forgetting those things which are behind and reaching forward to those things which are ahead" (Philippians 3:13) Paul exhorts us to focus on what God has for us in the future, and not hold onto the past, good or bad.

So what does God tell us?

"Do not remember the former things, nor consider the things of old. Behold, I will do a new thing. Now it shall spring forth; Shall you not know it? I will even make a road in the wilderness and rivers in the desert." (Isaiah 43:18-19)

Reminiscing is fun, and enjoying memories is great. But we must be careful that we don't get so caught up in the past, that we miss out on the future that God has for us.

"'For I know the thoughts that I think toward you' says the Lord, 'thoughts of peace and not of evil, to give you a future and a hope.'"* (Jeremiah 29:11) Isn't it exciting to know that God is thinking about you, and has a beautiful future planned out for you? Even more reason not to get caught up in the past!

REFLECTION TIME

Think about an "Egypt" moment in your life when you longed for something in the past. Discuss it here.

_____

_____

_____

_____

How has this situation hindered you from moving forward?

_____

_____

_____

_____

Look at Isaiah 43 from our study today. Commit this to memory. How does God having a "new thing" excite you and motivate you to keep on the path to your personal "promised land"?

_____

_____

_____

_____

Write out a prayer asking God to help you to leave the past behind, and to focus on committing to your walk with Him.

_____

_____

_____

_____

Dear Heavenly Father:

Thank you for your love, patience and grace. Sometimes we get so caught up the past and glamourizing it that we forget that Your plans for us are so much greater. The road will be tough sometimes, but we know that You will be with us every step of the way. Give us strength to endure when we get weary of the manna, knowing that we will eventually reach that promised land that You have for us if we keep our eyes and hearts on you. In Your precious name, Amen!

CALL TO ACTION!

Marching orders:

We all tend to hold on to memories of the "good old days". Is there something that you are holding onto that you need to let go of, so that you can be free to embrace the here and now? Search your heart and look for those "leeks and onions" longings the Israelites had. Write down one or two things and ask the Lord to help you let go of them, and to show you what He wants to fill the space with.

Ready, set, go!

I DON'T WANT TO GROW UP!

(Spiritual Maturity)

THERE'S A SPECIAL FREEDOM IN being a child. The responsibilities are few, and so are the worries. Children are not burdened with the mortgage payment, providing for the family, or even keeping the boogie man away. That's dad's job! Playing and learning are the duties of a kid.

I remember growing up around a lot of kids. In the summer, my mom babysat her two sisters' kids (five in total) which were added to the five of us siblings. To say it was hectic is an understatement. Crazy was more like it. One set of cousins lived behind us. We had adjoining backyards with a gate, so we could all play in the two huge backyards. It was a blast. I think the goal for my mom was just for us not to kill each other, and for all kids to be safely returned home at the end of the day!

A I grew older, I hung out with my best friend every day. We would ride bikes all around the neighborhood. Life was easier back then, and safer as well. We could walk anywhere and feel safe, and often did. Sadly, I think the innocence of childhood has been lost over the years.

But, alas, the time to grow up eventually arrived. Plans of college, career choices, adult responsibilities loomed over us. What are we going to do with our lives? Do we get a college degree or go right into the workforce? Decisions about marriage, family, and a house have replaced the dilemma of what game to play today-baseball or tag?

As Christians, we face the same path. We start out as "newbies", excited about our new-found faith, being immature about our knowledge of God's Word, and what is expected of us as we walk with Jesus. Many believers choose to stay at that level, not interested in growing mature in their faith. This was an issue that the Apostle Paul dealt with. Here are some of his admonishments:

"For though by this time you ought to be teachers, you need someone to teach you again the first principles of the oracles of God; and you have come to need milk and not solid food. For everyone who partakes only of milk is unskilled in the word of righteousness, for he is a babe." (Hebrews 5:11-13) Paul was rebuking the Hebrews for not having matured in their faith. They had been receiving instruction long enough to be able to teach the Word themselves. It is important that we be growing in our understanding of God's Word. Otherwise we are targets of deceiving spirits.

"And I, brethren, could not speak to you as to spiritual people but as to carnal, as to babes in Christ. I fed you with milk and not with solid food; for until now you were not able to receive it, and even now you are still not able; for you are still carnal. For where there are envy, strife, and divisions among you, are you not carnal and behaving like mere men?" (1 Corinthians 3:1-3) As he did with the Hebrews, Paul is admonishing the Corinthians for being immature in their faith, because of their carnal flesh. We need to be careful that we don't allow our behavior to stunt our spiritual growth.

Jesus addressed the same issue with the disciples, but not with chastisement. They were just not yet ready to comprehend all that was coming down the pike:

"I still have many things to say to you, but you cannot bear them now. However, when He, the Spirit of truth, has come, He will guide you into all truth; for He will not speak on His own authority, but whatever He hears He will speak; and He will tell you things to come." (John 16:12-13) Jesus knew the disciples were not mature enough to hear what He wanted to say. But He was preparing them for the coming of the Holy Spirit who would guide them. Paul sets a great example of the attitude we should adopt:

"Not that I have already attained, or am already perfected; but I press on, that I may lay hold of that for which Christ Jesus has also laid hold of me. Brethren, I do not count myself to have apprehended; but one thing I do, forgetting those things which are behind and reaching forward to those things which are ahead, I press toward the goal for the prize of the upward call of God in Christ Jesus." (Philippians 3:12-14) It should be the goal of every Christian to not be content with where we are at, but to always desire to strive toward Jesus, and to want everything He has for us.

"Brethren, do not be children in understanding; however, in malice be babes, but in understanding be mature." (1 Corinthians 14:20) Paul is exhorting us to be mature in our thinking, but do not allow ourselves to be drawn in by evil and harmful things.

"When I was a child, I spoke as a child, I understood as a child, I thought as a child; but when I became a man, I put away childish things." (1 Corinthians 13:11). There is a time for childlike behavior, and then there is a time to be a mature adult. This also applies in our Christian walk.

"And so, from the day we heard, we have not ceased to pray for you, asking that you may be filled with the knowledge of His will in all spiritual wisdom and understanding, so as to walk in a manner worthy of the Lord, fully pleasing to Him, bearing fruit in every good work and increasing in the knowledge of God." (Colossians 1:9-10) This is a prayer that we should all gladly receive.

There is a time in each of our lives as Christians when we need to decide how deeply we want to grow in our walk with Jesus. Personally, I have found a great excitement when I discover a new meaning to a passage, or a fresh insight to what He wants for me.

Our walk with Jesus is not something that we should play at, happily skipping along in ignorance. But rather something that is to be treasured; and treated as the unbelievable gift that it is. Growing in our knowledge of God's Word will draw us to a deeper and more intimate relationship; and will help us navigate this crazy thing called life.

"And let the peace of God rule in your hearts, to which also you were called in one body; and be thankful. Let the word of Christ dwell in you richly in all wisdom, teaching and admonishing one another in psalms, hymns and spiritual songs, singing with grace in your hearts to the Lord." (Colossians 3:15-16)

REFLECTION TIME

Think about how long you have been walking with the Lord. Do you feel that you have matured in your faith, or are you still a "babe" in the Word?

_____

_____

_____

_____

If you aren't satisfied with your level of growth, what do you think has hindered you, and how would you rectify that?

_____

_____

_____

_____

No matter how long we have been a Christian, we could never fully learn God's Word this side of heaven. How does Philippians 3 above encourage you to increase your knowledge of the Word?

_____

_____

_____

_____

Write out a prayer asking the Holy Spirit to help you to learn and comprehend what God has to show you through His Word.

_____

_____

_____

_____

Dear Heavenly Father:

Thank You for Your Word. Thank you that it has been given us to teach, exhort, correct, encourage, convict us, and to make us more like You. Sometimes when we read it, we have difficulty understanding or applying it. We ask that you empower the Holy Spirit to interpret and teach us so that we can live a life that is pleasing to You. We know that we will never be able to fully understand it in this mortal life, but we look forward to the day when it all will be revealed to us! In Your strong name, Amen!

CALL TO ACTION!

Marching orders:

Meditate on the level of your spiritual maturity. Seek the Lord, then write out a plan in your journal the steps you are going to take to grow deeper in your faith. Having a concrete plan will help you reach your goals.

Ready, set, go!

SPIRITUAL B.O.

(The Sweet Aroma of Jesus)

THE SENSE OF SMELL IS very powerful. It can conjure up all kinds of memories, some pleasant, and some not so much.

I was out driving one summer day and stopped in this little shopping center. It was quiet and on the warm side that morning. When I got out of my car, I smelled something cooking that took me right back to my mom's kitchen. She used to cook green beans with bacon on the stove for hours. I got this picture of a summer afternoon when I was sitting on the counter and mom had put a pan of beans on to simmer, and the aroma of the beans filled the kitchen. A great summer memory!

Here's another story. I used to manage a mom-and-pop Christian bookstore in Southern California. In the next city to the north, in the downtown area, there was a gift shop that was owned by a Wiccan. Every Wednesday, since I only worked half day, I would stop there on my way home. I would grab my Bible and a cup of coffee and sit out on the bench a few doors down, and would pray against the evils of the store, for the owner, and for all who went in and out. The smell of the incense would drift down my way. I always felt it was like Satan taunting me. So, I would pray harder. Well one day, I was at work and smelled this very familiar odor. I couldn't place it at first. Then I realized it was the exact same smell coming out of the gift shop! My heart flip-flopped and I exclaimed, "Satan is in the store!"' Talk about fervent prayers! Interestingly, the odor immediately disappeared.

Here is a rather unpleasant story, hence the title of the devotional. Almost a lifetime ago, when I was in my early twenties, I taught exercise classes. The owner had a racquetball club and decided to create a classroom upstairs above the weight room. It was a small gym, so there wasn't much air circulation. When the guys really got going downstairs, eventually the pungent smell of body sweat would drift upstairs. I am not fond of this smell. It grosses me out. And sorry, ladies, but it wasn't just the guys. There was a time when I had some visitors who added to the pungency in the room. You get my drift...right? lol

Some smells can be pleasing, and others repulsive. I think we can give off spiritual odors as well. Our attitude, our words, our actions all send a positive or negative message to those around us. An aroma if you will.

The Bible speaks of being an aroma to those who we are in contact with. First, the good:

"Now thanks be to God who always leads us in triumph in Christ, and through us diffuses the fragrance of His knowledge in every place. For we are to God the fragrance of Christ among those who are being saved and among those who are perishing. To the one we are the aroma of death leading to death, and to the other the aroma of life leading to life." (2 Corinthians 2:14-16) For those who do not believe, we are bringing news of doom to them. But to the believer, it is the sweet aroma of life with Jesus! Notice we are the diffusers. We are the vessels through which the fragrance of Jesus flows.

"And walk in love, as Christ also has loved us and given Himself for us, an offering and a sacrifice to God for a sweet-smelling aroma." (Ephesians 5:2) An offering is anything given to God. A sacrifice has the additional element of death. When we walk and love as Jesus did, and die to self, we become a pleasing aroma to God.

And then there's the not-so-good:

"Brood of vipers! How can you, being evil, speak good things? For out of the abundance of the heart the mouth speaks." (Matthew 12:34) Jesus was

chastising the Pharisees. Hearts filled with goodness will produce good things, but a heart full of hate will produce evil things. Those destructive thoughts become our words. And the result is stinky to the Lord. Spiritual bad breath!

"'To what purpose is the multitude of your sacrifices to Me?' says the Lord. 'I have had enough of burnt offerings of rams and the fat of fed cattle. I do not delight in the blood of bulls, or of lambs or goats. When you come to appear before Me, who has required this from your hand, to trample My courts? Bring no more futile sacrifices; incense is an abomination to Me.'" (Isaiah 1:11-13) In this passage, God is judging Judah and Jerusalem. Their sacrifices were empty because of the rampant sin they were involved in. We must also be sure that we are coming to the Lord with pure hearts and motives. Otherwise, the aroma of the sacrifice is a stench to Him.

Paul had some complimentary things to say to the Philippian church:

"Indeed, I have all and abound. I am full, having received from Epaphroditus the things sent from you, a sweet-smelling aroma, an acceptable sacrifice, well pleasing to God." (Philippians 4:18) The sacrificial gift that was given to Paul, which came from love, was most pleasing to God as well. Our heartfelt sacrifices to each other can reach all the way to heaven!

It's interesting how much time and money we spend on smelling good. Deodorants, mouthwash, perfumes, scented this and that, all because we do not want to be offensive to others. But a more vital area we need to be presenting comes from the heart. Our attitudes, actions, words, deeds, all done in a Christ-like manner produce a sweet aroma to Jesus. On the other hand, those done out of self-serving motives are a stench to Him. And He is most displeased with this.

So, grab your spiritual soap, which is the Word of God. Learn of Him, emulate Him, as He humbly washed the feet of His disciples (read John 13). And be like Peter, and say "wash all of me, Lord!" Then we will be a sweet-smelling aroma to our Lord and Savior. Squeaky clean from head to toe, inside and out!

REFLECTION TIME

Take a moment and think about the aroma you have been giving off lately. What specifically has been giving off a stench?

_____

_____

_____

_____

If you could go back and correct that behavior or attitude, what would you change?

_____

_____

_____

_____

Meditate on the passage from 2 Corinthians 2:14-16. How can you be a "diffuser" of the fragrance of Jesus to those you encounter daily? Are there ways you can change in how you represent God?

_____

_____

_____

_____

Write out a prayer asking God to help you rid your heart of the stinky stuff you are carrying around, and to fill it with the sweet aroma of our Lord.

_____

_____

_____

_____

Dear Heavenly Father:

Thank you that You are a sweet fragrance. Help us to be more like You, giving off a pleasing aroma, rather than an offensive stench. We know that our actions and attitudes and ultimately our words come from the abundance of our hearts. When that is right, then we are pleasing to You. When it is not, then we are an offense to You. Help us to know that the gospel is an offense to one who is perishing, but if we present it in the light of Your heart, then we have done a good thing. Keep us strong and focused on leading a life that You would have us lead. In Your name, Amen!

CALL TO ACTION!

Marching orders:

Take a look at the aroma you are giving off to others, spiritually speaking. Think specifically of an incident in the past week where you either gave off the scent of Jesus, or stunk up the place. Or maybe one of each! What did you do or say that pleased the Lord, and what did you do or say that displeased Him? Journal your thoughts about how your heart can give off that sweet aroma of Jesus. Ask Him to reveal those stinky places!

Ready, set, go!

EENY, MEENY, MINY, MO

(Choosing the Right Path)

LIFE IS A CONSTANT BARRAGE of choices. From the moment we get up in the morning until we go to bed, we are making decisions. Most of them we don't even think about. We just do them. Like breathing!

Remember back to your childhood. Did you and your friends decide what to do by using the "eeny meeny" rhyme? Or maybe you settled differences with the "rock, paper, scissors" game (which sadly, some adults are still doing this!). Drawing straws is another favorite. Short stick always loses.

Unfortunately, we can't go through life making decisions based on childhood games. Nor can we be swayed by popular opinion or snazzy advertising gimmicks. I honestly believe there are people who choose how they are going to vote on a candidate or a proposition by the number of yard signs or flyers in their mail. That's how advertisers make their mark. Put it in front of your face enough times, it will get your attention.

Life-impacting decisions need to be carefully thought out, researched and prayed about. You can't choose a college based on the party scene. Or choose a career path simply because of the income potential. It must be a right fit for your gifts, talents, and passion.

There is one life decision that has an impact far greater than we can imagine. It is the decision whether to follow Jesus. This is a choice that will not only impact our lives here on this earth, but our eternal destination. We are essentially choosing life or death, heaven or hell, eternal joy or eternal damnation. Let me tell you, eternity is a long time!

The Bible is clear about what each path will offer. Where Jesus is truth, life, and everlasting joy, Satan is nothing but deception, lies, and the attempt to destroy your life and very soul. Let's look at the differences through the lens of scripture:

"The thief does not come except to steal, and to kill, and to destroy. I have come that they may have life, and that they may have it more abundantly." (John 10:10). This is the clearest scripture, in my opinion about the difference between Jesus and Satan.

"Every good gift and every perfect gift is from above, and comes down from the Father of lights, with whom there is no variation or shadow of turning." (James 1:17) Jesus only has good things for us. He will not sway from this. Satan taunts us with promises of good, but only delivers evil.

"What then? Shall we sin because we are not under law but under grace? Certainly not! Do you not know that to whom you present yourselves slaves to obey, you are that one's slaves whom you obey, whether of sin leading to death, or of obedience leading to righteousness?" (Romans 6:15-16) Again, we are making a choice whom we are following. We are either going to be a slave to Satan by leading a life of sin, or a slave to Jesus, by leading a life of righteousness.

"See, I have set before you today life and good, death and evil, in that I command you today to love the Lord your God, to walk in His ways, and to keep His commandments, His statutes, and His judgments, that you may live and multiply; and the Lord your God will bless you in the land which you go to possess. But if your heart turns away so that you do not hear, and are drawn away, and worship other gods and serve them, I announce to you today that you shall surely perish; you shall not prolong your days in the land which you cross over the Jordan to go in and possess. I call heaven

and earth as witnesses today against you, that I have set before you, life and death, blessing and cursing; therefore, choose life, that both you and your descendants may live." (Deuteronomy 30:15-19) God was speaking through Moses to the Israelites. But we can apply this to our lives today. If we choose to walk in the ways of God, we will be blessed and will receive life. But if we choose idols and evil things (and anything can be an idol if it takes the place of God in our hearts) we are warned that there will be death and cursings. Being separated eternally from Jesus is the only alternative we have if we reject Him. And it is a horrific choice with dire consequences.

"He who rejects Me, and does not receive My words, has that which judges him—the word that I have spoken will judge him in the last day" (John 12:48). The Lord has given us His Word. He has called us to Him. He has provided us with Bibles, pastors, teachers, and evangelists to proclaim His message of repentance and everlasting life. If we reject His message, we will have no excuse to offer Him at the day of judgment. And then it will be too late anyways. We need to seek Him while we can find Him.

"Now therefore, fear the Lord, serve Him in sincerity and in truth, and put away the gods which your fathers served on the other side of the River and in Egypt. Serve the Lord! And if it seems evil to you to serve the Lord, choose for yourselves this day whom you will serve, whether the gods which your fathers served that were on the other side of the River, or the gods of the Amorites, in whose land you dwell. But as for me and my house, we will serve the Lord." (Joshua 24:14-15) Joshua is challenging the Israelites to essentially give up the idols they were still serving. The last line is the declaration we all should make as followers of Jesus Christ.

Many years ago, I worked with a gal who had recently become a Christian. She said something that saddened me. In speaking of her decision to follow Christ she declared, "I'm in, I'm just not ALL the way in." With a big emphasis on the word "all". Folks, I am here to tell you this: being a follower of Jesus Christ is not a hobby, where we commit just as far as our interests go. It is not a part time, compartmentalized aspect of our life. He wants all of us, 24/7. We are either with Him or against Him. (Matthew 12:30)

So, if you find yourself standing at a fork in the road, consider the words of Jesus. You can either go to the one side and follow down the crooked path of destruction or choose the path of Jesus. If you are not sure what that road looks like, search the scriptures, and He will direct your path.

"Your word is a lamp to my feet and a light to my path." (Psalm 119:105)

"And you will seek Me and find Me, when you search for Me with all your heart." Jeremiah 29:13)

REFLECTION TIME

Think back to when you made the decision to follow Jesus. What was that moment like for you? Did you fully understand the commitment?

_____

_____

_____

_____

Decisions can be extremely difficult to make. Was there one recently that you sought the Lord for guidance (or failed to seek Him)? How was your decision impacted by your choice to seek His counsel?

_____

_____

_____

_____

Meditate on Deuteronomy 30:15-19. Do you have idols that may be hindering your entering into your personal promised land? How are you choosing them over a full life with Jesus?

_____

_____

_____

_____

Write out a prayer asking God to open your eyes to the wrong choices you have made. Ask Him to guide you back onto the right path.

_____

_____

_____

Dear Heavenly Father:

There are so many things in our daily lives that can distract us from walking in Your light. Satan is constantly barraging us with shiny objects that capture our attention and entice us with false promises. Help us to recognize this when it happens and to turn to You for protection, strength, and the courage to abstain from the lies he taunts us with. Show us how to navigate this world and walk strongly in Your truth. In Your Strong name, Amen!

CALL TO ACTION!

Marching orders:

Journal time again. Picture this vision in your mind. You are standing at a fork in the road in this beautiful forest setting. The sign marker has two directions. To the left, it says "Everything your heart desires on this earth-an easy hike". To the right it says, "Your Promised Land-caution lots of hills and valleys". What are you feeling as you stand there? You need to be totally honest with yourself. What are the benefits and sacrifices you would experience going down each path? Ask yourself this question-are the rewards of choosing one road worth the sacrifice of the other road? In other words, count the cost of each road. What is your decision? Give this a lot of thought.

Ready, set, go!

I'M TOO BUSY RIGHT NOW!

(Seeking the Peace of God)

WE LIVE IN A WORLD that is so fast paced that we don't seem to be able to breathe, let alone stop and smell the roses. We run here and there, like rats in a maze. I read a study recently that 82% of Americans report moderate to high levels of stress in their job. Deadlines, understaffed departments, overbearing bosses, unrealistic expectations and budget cuts all lead to an unhealthy environment. And to think we do this five days a week!

I remember a few years ago, I was searching for a new place to live. The landlord had told my roommate and me that he was likely to be selling the townhouse sometime in the future. Even though it wasn't definite, I went on a mad search to find a place. The Lord had spoken to me for a while through Psalm 46:10, ***"Be still and know that I am God."*** I was hearing it everywhere, even to the point that my friends would look at me and smile if it came up in church. I have a picture of a beautiful snow scene with the scripture on it. I see total peace and tranquility in the picture. I can almost hear the quiet.

Anyway, I was obsessing about finding a new apartment, even though I didn't know for sure when I had to move, if at all. But that didn't stop me. As I said, I was hearing this scripture everywhere, but I didn't heed the direction. So God, with His special humor, decided to be creative in reaching me. One day, while perusing the housing market, I clicked on a rental unit. As I clicked the various pictures of the place, I noticed that in the bathroom, right over the toilet, was the same picture hanging on the wall that I had! I guess God figured, if He couldn't get me to stop obsessing by using my surroundings, He would go right into the obsession itself!

Jesus longs for us to sit at His feet and just be with Him. You might remember the story of Mary and Martha, two sisters who both loved Jesus. When He came to visit them, Martha, the perfect hostess, was busy making sure all the practical needs were being met in preparing dinner for their guest. Mary, however, chose to sit at the feet of Jesus and listen to His teaching. This ticked Martha off, and she even complained to Jesus about it. Not exactly proper dinner hostess etiquette to complain to the guest. Here's the passage:

"Now it happened as they went that He entered a certain village; and a certain woman named Martha welcomed Him into her house. And she had a sister called Mary, who also sat at Jesus' feet and heard His word. But Martha was distracted with much serving, and she approached Him and said, 'Lord, do You not care that my sister has left me to serve alone? Therefore, tell her to help me.' And Jesus answered and said to her, 'Martha, Martha, you are worried and troubled about many things. But one thing is needed, and Mary has chosen that good part, which will not be taken away from her.'" (Luke 10:38-42)

Not exactly the response Martha wanted, I am sure. But what He was telling her was that He valued affection over service. We need to be careful that we don't get caught up in the service part of our relationship with Jesus that we neglect the affection and interaction with the Lord.

Have you ever heard this family dynamic? (Maybe it's a reality in your own home.) Dad is so busy working to provide for his family-a nice house, clothes, food, two cars, a private school education, that he is neglecting a very important part of his role as dad- to be with the family, to just love on them, have a catch in the backyard. We can't ignore the good part, as Jesus called it. So how do we get off this treadmill that keeps us running and running? We heed the Word of God:

"Come to Me, all you who labor and are heavy laden, and I will give you rest. Take My yoke upon you and learn from Me, for I am gentle and lowly in heart, and you will find rest for your souls. For My yoke is easy and My burden is light." (Matthew 11:28-30) When we are overburdened, we need to come to Jesus, and lay our yoke upon Him and take up His, which is a life of submission. Then He is in control of all the chaos. He will give us the rest and peace that we need.

"Do not overwork to be rich; because of your own understanding, cease!" (Proverbs 23:4) Are you striving to gain more possessions? Are you missing out on what God has for you in order to achieve "just a little more"?

"But seek first the kingdom of God and His righteousness, and all these things shall be added to you. Therefore, do not worry about tomorrow, for tomorrow will worry about its own things. Sufficient for the day is its own trouble." (Matthew 6:33-34) Put all things before God. Quite possibly those things you are worrying about may not even happen. Or if they do, He will make your way easier.

"Rest in the Lord and wait patiently for Him; do not fret because of him who prospers in his way, because of the man who brings wicked schemes to pass." (Psalm 37:7) Jesus is carrying your burden, so you don't need to carry it as well. Just wait on Him and let go of anything that is causing you anxiety or stress.

Practically speaking, how do we do this? We can't just give up our job because it is stressful. We still need to carry on in this world. May I suggest that you carve out a time for just you and the Lord? A few minutes in the Word before getting started with your day, a lunchtime break with Jesus, quiet time with Him at the end of the day. However, you need or choose to do it, make it a priority. He is longing to hear from you. He wants to pour out His love on you. But if you don't make a space for that to happen, He won't force Himself on you. He may create a situation that opens the door for that, but ultimately the choice is yours whether you want to seek Him or not. I highly recommend that you do!

By the way, this lack of time with Jesus can happen to you even if you are retired and not encumbered with anything. Filling your time with busyness is just as distracting. Think about it!

"Oh, taste and see that the Lord is good; blessed is the man who trusts in Him!" (Psalm 34:8) Better than a box of Godiva chocolate!

REFLECTION TIME

Take a moment and think about the pace of your life. Do you feel that you are running full speed on a treadmill? If so, what are some things that maybe the Lord has asked you to give up or scale back on?

_____

_____

_____

_____

What are some practical things you can do to create more real and intimate time with Jesus? If you have a family, involve them in this as well.

_____

_____

_____

_____

Are you a Mary or a Martha? How does that look in your day-to-day life?

_____

_____

_____

_____

Choose one of today's scriptures. How does it speak to you? Write out a prayer asking God to help you implement the exhortation.

_____

_____

_____

_____

Dear Heavenly Father:

We are such busy people these days, running here and there, trying to get everything on our to-do list accomplished. But we know that there are many things on that list that are not needful; activities and responsibilities that You would have us say no to. Lord, would you help us to discern what You consider to be a distraction, much like Martha experienced? We don't want anything to take us away from enjoying that intimate, precious time at Your feet. Help us to be like Mary and choose the good part. Help us to be still and know that You are God. In Your precious name, Amen!

CALL TO ACTION!

Marching orders:

Get your day planner out. Pencil in (better yet, write it in ink!) a specific time you are going to sit down and spend 15 minutes alone at the feet of Jesus. Just be still, don't ask for anything, just receive. Offer up your praises to Him. Thank Him for all that He is and does. Grab a journal and write down the experience of what that time with Him was like. Commit to this every day. At the end of the first week, write in your journal the impact it had on your relationship with Him. I know you can do this. Turn off the TV, shut down the internet, go into your bedroom and close the door. Just get away from everyone and everything. You will survive being unplugged for 15 minutes. I promise!

Ready, set, go!

AN ATTITUDE OF GRATITUDE
(A Time of Thanksgiving)

THANKSGIVING IS JUST A FEW days away. It is my favorite time of the year. When I was a kid, we had huge Thanksgiving dinners. Mom would put the turkey on at the crack of dawn. She would spend all day cooking. It was a veritable feast! We helped of course. I had certain jobs that I did each year. I would mix the pumpkin pie filling, chop carrots, peel and chop the yams, and butter the tops of the homemade rolls, which were to die for! We had traditional dishes-turkey with homemade dressing, carrots, sweet potatoes with pineapple and brown sugar, cranberry relish, and our choice of pumpkin or apple pie to round off the meal. Sometimes even custard pie. The entire family came over. After we were totally stuffed, we sat around the table and played a game or two of cards. Great memories.

Commercialism has crept into the holiday season. I saw a cartoon that summed up my entire feeling. There were 3 cars on a road. The car on the left had a jack-o-lantern driving, the car on the right had Santa driving, and the car in the middle was a turkey. All three cars were converging, with Santa crossing over all lanes. The caption read, spoken from the Halloween car, "Stay in your own lane!" The poor turkey was getting squeezed out from both sides. That is what it has come down to. The commercialism of it all. Halloween, which used to be a day, is now called a season (one I personally could do without…). Christmas products start arriving in the stores barely after school has started in the fall, and Thanksgiving has been relegated to just a day to stuff our faces. Do you remember when Black Friday was the day after Thanksgiving, and all the stores were closed on Thursday, but opened super early Friday? Now, Black Friday is a block of time that starts three weeks before the traditional day, and only a handful of stores bother to close on Thanksgiving. They might miss their piece of the money pie.

My fear is that we have forgotten how to be thankful. We live in an era of entitlement, that we are simply getting what society owes us. We need to be thankful that God, in His grace and mercy, doesn't give us what we really deserve. But that's a discussion for another day.

Rather than taking for granted all the things God has done or provided, let's look to His Word, and explore some scriptures on gratitude:

"Oh, give thanks to the Lord, for He is good! For His mercy endures forever." (1 Chronicles 16:34) Ah, mercy-God's gift of compassion and kindness. He is withholding punishment for that we deserve, if we are true believers.

"Oh, that men would give thanks to the Lord for His goodness, and for His wonderful works to the children of men! For He satisfies the longing soul, and fills the hungry soul with goodness." (Psalm 107:8-9) Just reading that passage gives me peace in my heart!

We are commanded to give thanks to God. Since we are people who don't like to be told what to do, how can we do this with a willing heart?

"Make a joyful shout to the Lord, all you lands! Serve the Lord with gladness; come before His presence with singing. Know that the Lord, He is God; It is He who has made us, and not we ourselves; we are His people and the sheep of His pasture. Enter into His gates with thanksgiving, and into His courts with praise. Be thankful to Him, and bless His name. For the Lord is good; His mercy is everlasting, and His truth endures to all generations." (Psalm 100) This is the psalm in its entirety. Small, but packed with goodness. We are given eight actions to engage in to give praise to our Lord and Savior. If we approach our Lord with hearts like this, we cannot help but praise Him!

"The sting of death is sin, and the strength of sin is the law. But thanks be to God, who gives us the victory through our Lord Jesus Christ." (1 Corinthians 15:57) Our faith in Jesus has given us victory over death and sin. Now that's something to be thankful for!

What should we thank Him for? We need to go beyond just thank you for all the good things He does for us.

"In everything give thanks; for this is the will of God in Christ Jesus for you." (1 Thessalonians 5:18) Everything that we have we owe to God. And guess what? Even the trials are something that we can thank Him for because through them, if we remember His sovereignty, we will grow closer to Him, mature spiritually, or minister to another person who is suffering.

"In this you greatly rejoice, though now for a little while, if need be, you have been grieved by various trials, that the genuineness of your faith, being much more precious than gold that perishes, though it is tested by fire, may be found to praise, honor, and glory at the revelation of Jesus Christ, whom having not seen you love. Though now you do not see Him, yet believing, you rejoice with joy inexpressible and full of glory, receiving the end of your faith—the salvation of your souls." (1 Peter 1:6-9) There is no trial on earth that can compare to the riches of heaven. Hold onto that belief, even through the roughest of storms. He will make it right in His perfect timing.

As followers of Christ, being thankful should be an automatic response to everything in our lives. We have got to be careful not to take for granted all that He has given us and done for us. Our gratitude and adoration of Him pales in comparison to what He offers us. Let us not lose sight of this. Giving thanks one day of the year has no place in the thoughts and hearts of a believer.

"We give You thanks, O Lord God Almighty, the One who is and who was and who is to come." (Revelation 11:17a)

Thank you, Jesus!

REFLECTION TIME

Think back to some of your family Thanksgiving traditions. Did they include a time of prayer and thanksgiving or was the attitude, "Let's eat!"

_____

_____

_____

_____

Have you cultivated an attitude of gratitude, or has that part of your walk been a little anemic lately?

_____

_____

_____

_____

Reflect on Psalm 100, and the exhortations in it. Make a course of action in how you are going to incorporate these into your daily walk.

_____

_____

_____

_____

Write out a prayer of thanksgiving. Just take time to praise Him and thank Him for all He has done and will do in your life.

_____

_____

_____

_____

Dear Heavenly Father:

We have so much to be thankful for. We could spend the rest of our lives thanking You, and I don't think we could exhaust the list. Help us to never take You or Your goodness for granted. The sacrifice You made so we could be spared from eternal separation is more than we can even imagine. We are so unworthy, yet You love us with an unending and unfailing love. That is mind-blowing. To You be all the praise and the glory. In Your precious name, Amen!

CALL TO ACTION!

Marching orders:

Using a journal or a notebook, each day for the next 30 days, I am challenging you to write down 5 things that you are thankful to the Lord for. Each day needs to be different. So at the end of the challenge, you will have 150 different things that you are thankful for! Who knew?? You've got this, my friend!

Ready, set, go!

I ONCE WAS BLIND

(Spiritual Eyesight)

VISION IS AN INCREDIBLE THING. Being able to see the beauty of what is around us is a gift from God. I think if I had to lose one of my senses, vision would be the hardest. I have noticed, though, as I am growing older, it's a little harder (understatement) to see the fine print. My eyes fatigue easier than they used to. I have those reader cheaters all over the house. I say all over, because I tend to leave them wherever I am, which causes me to spend a great deal of time looking for them! Grrr....

We have a different kind of vision as well. You guessed it, spiritual vision. But this isn't something we are born with; it must be developed. Interestingly, this is a vision that we are in total control of. No disease or accident can take it away from us, unless we allow it to. It's a type of vision that we make the decision to use or not.

Have you ever been in total darkness? I mean, where you literally cannot see a thing. When I lived in another area up here, it was in a more rural setting. There were no city lights, or "light pollution" as they call it. On a clear night, you can see a million stars. Well, one night the power went out, and let me tell you it was darker than dark! Pitch black would be a good description. All I could think of is this what the Bible means when it speaks of outer darkness?? Whoa! That would have scared me into repentance if I weren't already a believer. But guess what? All I had to do was turn on my flashlight, and voila, I had light.

The Bible speaks of light vs dark. First, let's explore what it says about Jesus:

"In Him was life, and the life was the light of men. And the light shines in the darkness, and the darkness did not comprehend it." (John 1:4-5) John was describing Jesus. He can shine in the darkest caverns of our hearts and take away the darkness (sin).

"Then Jesus spoke to them again, saying, 'I am the light of the world. He who follows Me shall not walk in darkness but have the light of life.'" (John 8:12) Jesus is the light that prevails in this sinful world. If we follow Him, we can have victory over sin and darkness.

"The Lord is my light and my salvation; whom shall I fear? The Lord is the strength of my life; of whom shall I be afraid?" (Psalm 27:1) God is our light and strength in our darkest hour. With Him, we don't need to be afraid of anything or anyone.

How are we spiritually blind? Satan desires to keep us in the darkness, to keep us from seeing the light, and being freed from the bondage of sin. When we are in spiritual darkness, we don't want to hear the gospel, believe on Jesus Christ, and are easily lured into false beliefs.

"But even if our gospel is veiled, it is veiled to those who are perishing, whose minds the god of this age has blinded, who do not believe, lest the light of the gospel of the glory of Christ, who is the image of God, should shine on them." (2 Corinthians 4:3-4) The god of this age is Satan, and he has put spiritual blinders on these people, so that they would perish in their sins.

"Go to this people and say: 'Hearing you will hear, and shall not understand; and seeing you will see, and not perceive; for the hearts of this people have grown dull. Their ears are hard of hearing, and their eyes they have closed, lest they should see with their eyes and hear with their ears, lest they should understand with their hearts and turn, so that I should heal them.'" (Acts 28:26-27) Paul's message of salvation was once again being rejected by the

Jewish nation. He is quoting Isaiah 6:9-10. With dull hearts, closed ears and eyes, we cannot comprehend the message of the gospel.

"For the message of the cross is foolishness to those who are perishing, but to us who are being saved it is the power of God." (1 Corinthians 1:18) People with worldly wisdom decry the gospel as pure folly, but for believers it has the power to save.

Removal of spiritual blinders:

It is possible for these blinders and earplugs to be removed. It is the simple process of choosing to receive the gospel. The shackles will be removed, and we will see the truth. God removed the scales from Paul's eyes (he was a staunch Pharisee, hater of Jews), and used him mightily to evangelize both Jew and Gentile:

"I will deliver you from the Jewish people, as well as from the Gentiles, to whom I now send you, to open their eyes, in order to turn them from darkness to light, and from the power of Satan to God, that they may receive forgiveness of sins and an inheritance among those who are sanctified by faith in Me." (Acts 26:17-18) God used Paul in a powerful way to spread the message of salvation. But he needed to go through a conversion process himself!

There is a fabulous exchange between a blind man whom Jesus healed and the Pharisees who refused to believe that Jesus was God, but instead accused Him of being a sinner (Read John chapter 9). The blind man summed it up perfectly:

"He answered and said, 'Whether He is a sinner or not I do not know. One thing I know: that though I was blind, now I see.'" (John 9:25). All the blind man knew was, at that moment, he followed the direction of Jesus and had his sight restored. A later conversation with Jesus opened his spiritual eyes to believe that He was the Son of God.

God can open the spiritual eyes and ears of anyone who genuinely seeks Him. All it takes is a simple conversation. The heart can be softened, and the truth can be received. But there will be a point where the heart has become so hardened, that He won't open their eyes.

"Seek the Lord while He may be found, call upon Him while He is near. Let the wicked forsake his way, and the unrighteous man his thoughts; let him return to the Lord, and He will have mercy on him; and to our God, for He will abundantly pardon." (Isaiah 55:6-7)

REFLECTION TIME

We were all spiritually blind before we came to the Lord. Reflect on your personal time of conversion. How did the Lord orchestrate it?

_____

_____

_____

_____

Even as believers we can be spiritually blind or deaf. Is there an area in your walk with Jesus where He is showing you it needs to change, but you're not willing to obey?

_____

_____

_____

_____

Reflect on Psalm 27:1. How has knowing that God is your light and salvation given you courage or strength when you needed it?

_____

_____

_____

_____

Write out a prayer, thanking God for removing the blinders from your eyes. Ask Him to reveal any areas of your heart that are still blind or deaf to His calling in your life.

_____

_____

_____

Dear Heavenly Father:

Thank you that You love us so much that You desire that none of us should perish. Thank You for having made a way for us to have eternal life with You, and forgiveness of our sins. We are a stiff-necked people for sure! But we thank You for Your abundant mercy, grace, patience while we try to figure this out. I pray for all those who are currently blinded by the enemy. Pull the scales from their eyes, Lord. Guide them out of darkness and into Your marvelous light. In Your name, Amen!

CALL TO ACTION!

Marching orders:

Think of one person in your life who has spiritual blinders on. Commit to praying for him or her every day for at least one week. Ask God for an opportunity to share the gospel with that person, either verbally, or in a written note. And stand back so you don't get hit with the scales flying off!

Ready, set, go!

WHERE'S THE BEEF?

(Fast Food Spirituality)

HAVE YOU NOTICED HOW THE world seems to be going at a break-neck speed? Everyone's in such a hurry. People don't seem to want to slow down and get into the heart of things. They want everything quickly, wrapped up in a quick sound bite or brief headline. What happened to digging into something and immersing yourself in it, like a good book? Cliff notes, please!

Our attention span seems to be shrinking. If we must focus on anything for any length of time, we glaze over. I was watching a group of new hires the other day. The trainer was explaining the time clock procedures. And more than one of them were drifting away in their attention. If I could read their minds, it would probably be, "I wish I could check my phone right now!" We seem to be walking around with our heads in the clouds.

Do you remember the days of character-driven movies, with real story lines? Now, it's all flash and action. As for information, it's just the headlines, ma'am! And please bullet-point your message so I can just scan it.

I fear that the fast-food mentality is happening in the church today as well. The tendency for some churches is to pick a topic and sandwich a few verses around it to make a point. The time of the verse-by-verse teaching through the Bible is fading. I heard a pastor once say that he toured several churches in an area. He found, out of ten churches he visited, only two churches were teaching *from* the Bible, and only one was teaching *through* the Bible. If we are not learning the whole counsel of God, how can we properly navigate this Christian life? How do we get to know God, if we don't study His Word in its entirety? There are some churches who don't teach about prophecy, which is alarming, since about a third of the Bible is prophecy. Or let's not offend and teach about sin, hell, or that seven letter word-gasp- "tithing". We don't want to go too deep, lest we scare people away. What a shame!

Granted, I don't want to sit in a sanctuary, fidgeting because the preacher is going on and on, without saying a whole lot. But I do want some meat to chew on. That's the point, isn't it? If I don't walk out of there with something I can take home with me, or apply to my life, then I have pretty much wasted my time. I am not interested in "Christianity Lite"!

And with that in mind, what does the Bible say about digging deep into His Word?

"Whoever comes to Me, and hears My sayings and does them, I will show you whom he is like: He is like a man building a house, who dug deep and laid the foundation on the rock. And when the flood arose, the stream beat vehemently against that house, and could not shake it, for it was founded on the rock." (Luke 6:47-48) In order to stand strong in this world, we need to have a solid foundation in Jesus, who is our Rock. We can only get that by knowing what He says in His Word.

"All Scripture is given by inspiration of God, and is profitable for doctrine, for reproof, for correction, for instruction in righteousness, that the man of God may be complete, thoroughly equipped for every good work." (2 Timothy 3:16-17) Notice it says ALL scripture. We cannot receive the full benefit of God's Word if we are approaching it halfheartedly, or just scratching the surface.

"Be diligent to present yourself approved to God, a worker who does not need to be ashamed, rightly dividing the word of truth." (2 Timothy 2:15) To rightly divide the word means to handle it in the proper manner. To present it in truth, without falsifying it. Again, we can only do that if we know it. I like the King James version which says, "study to show yourself approved" unto God.

"Therefore, take up the whole armor of God, that you may be able to withstand in the evil day, and having done all, to stand. Stand therefore, having girded your waist with truth, having put on the breastplate of righteousness, and having shod your feet with the preparation of the gospel of peace; above all, taking the shield of faith with which you will be able to quench all the fiery darts of the wicked one. And take the helmet of salvation, and the sword of the Spirit, which is the word of God." (Ephesians 6:13-17). This passage describes every piece of spiritual armor we are to put on to protect us from the fiery darts of the enemy. Look at each one. How can you arm yourself with these, if you don't understand the Biblical truth of them?

"For the Word of God is living and powerful, and sharper than any two-edged sword, piercing even to the division of soul and spirit, and of joints and marrow, and is a discerner of the thoughts and intents of the heart." (Hebrews 4:12)

That's all well and good, you might say. I don't have time to sit down and really study the Bible beyond what I learn at church. I'd be willing to bet that if you really looked at how you spend your time, you would find that there is indeed time to spend in God's Word. Turn off the TV, shut off the internet and the phone for starters.

Maybe you would like to dig deeper, but you aren't sure how to start. May I make some suggestions for you? There are so many wonderful online bible study tools that will help you to understand the Word. Commentaries, Bible dictionaries, software. Today, it is right at your fingertips. Choose a book of the Bible and start reading it. Find a good commentary on it. Learn what the scriptures mean. Use the scriptures in these devotionals to further your understanding of them. I encourage you to not just read the passage, or my comments. But look up the passage and read the entire chapter. An inductive study approach is an excellent way to study the Bible. This is where you learn the who, where, what, why and how of things. Again, you can research inductive study methods on the internet.

By digging deep into God's Word, you will discover amazing nuggets that you will have missed just skimming the surface. Your walk with God will be so much more meaningful if you understand better what the Bible says. It is more personal than just a book that you read. It is His love letter to us. And it is all about Jesus, from Genesis to Revelation. Start studying, my friend!

REFLECTION TIME

Have you been to a church, (or maybe you attend one now) where you feel that there was no spiritual growth? What was their method of teaching like?

_____

_____

_____

_____

Think about areas in your walk that you need to grow in or understand better. Is it faith, grace, God's mercy? What are some ways that you can strengthen these areas?

_____

_____

_____

_____

Take a deeper look at Ephesians 6:13-17. Meditate on each piece of armor. Do a word study on each one. How do you feel this will protect you from the enemy, and draw you closer to God?

_____

_____

_____

Write a prayer asking for the power of the Holy Spirit to help you grow in your knowledge of God's Word. Ask Him to help you apply it, and have heart knowledge, not just head knowledge.

_____

_____

_____

Dear Heavenly Father:

Thank you for the power of Your Word. Forgive us for taking it so lightly. We ask that You help us to gain a deeper understanding so that we can know how to live a life according to Your will. Show us how to study and apply our newfound knowledge, and not have it just be something that we can quote or discuss. We need to learn how to live it out. We can only do this through the power of Your Holy Spirit. In Your name, Amen!

CALL TO ACTION!

Marching orders:

Choose a book of the Bible that you are going to commit to studying. You might want to start with a smaller one, like 1 John. Set aside a time that you are going to sit down every day and dig into it. I recommend the Inductive study method. www.precept.org has several resources and study guidebooks that will be invaluable to your Biblical education. Happy studying!

Ready, set, go!

NOT SO, LORD!

(Commander or Lieutenant?)

WE LIVE IN A SELF-SUFFICIENT society, with a "doing it my way" attitude. Years ago, there was a hamburger chain slogan, "Have it your way". That's what we want to do-call all the shots.

But what if we were all leaders, and there were no followers? It could make for a chaotic situation. Everybody doing things the way they want, and nobody working together. That's why we have rules and regulations. This calls for submission on our part. To our employer, law enforcement officers, parents, teachers. Can you imagine a military attack with no commander in charge?? It wouldn't work if some said, "No, I don't like that plan. I want to do it this way." What was one of the first words we all learned as babies? NO!!! Nobody had to teach us to be defiant.

The Bible calls for us to be submissive to the Lord and His precepts. Yes, I know that although the old testament was under the law, the new testament is under grace. But that doesn't change what God is requiring of us.

"Therefore, submit to God. Resist the devil and he will flee from you." (James 4:7) We cannot take on Satan ourselves. It must be done in the name of Jesus; through His power working in us.

"He knelt down and prayed, saying, "Father, if it is Your will, take this cup away from Me; nevertheless, not My will, but Yours, be done." (Luke 22:41-

42) Jesus was the ultimate example of total submission to His Father's will. If He did it, where do we have the audacity to say No?

"Therefore, humble yourselves under the mighty hand of God, that He may exalt you in due time." (1 Peter 5:6) God resists the proud; and refusing to submit to Him stems from pride. Humility allows God to work in our lives and hearts.

"Because the carnal mind is enmity against God; for it is not subject to the law of God, nor indeed can be." (Romans 8:7). Enmity is being hostile or opposed to something. The rebellious heart has no place in a Christian's life.

Sometimes we want to put God at the back of the line. We say we want to be obedient, submissive, a servant. That we want God to be in control of our lives. But when we are in the trenches, how often we move God from Commander to Lieutenant, and ask Him to follow us! We may not do this consciously, but we do it. The Apostle Peter, who loved the Lord, and was a follower of His, referred to Jesus as Lord. This is a submissive position. But three separate times he called Him Lord, then rebuked Jesus!

First rebuke:

This is typical of human nature, and I am glad that God included it in the Bible. Peter has just declared that Jesus is the Son of the living God. Then when Jesus is telling them of His crucifixion, Peter responded, *"Then Peter took Him aside and began to rebuke Him, saying, "Far be it from You, Lord; this shall not happen to You!"* (Matthew 16:22)

Second rebuke:

"Peter, who said to him, 'Lord, are you going to wash my feet?' Jesus replied, 'You do not realize now what I am doing, but later you will understand.' 'No" said Peter, *you shall never wash my feet. Jesus answered, Unless I wash you, you have no part with me.'"* (John 13:6-8) I love Peter's response, "Wash all of me, Lord!"

Third rebuke:

"And a voice came to him, 'Rise, Peter; kill and eat.' But Peter said, 'Not so, Lord! For I have never eaten anything common or unclean.' And a voice spoke to him again the second time, 'What God has cleansed you must not call common.'" (Acts 10:13-15) Not so, Lord?? That's brazen.

Before we become too critical of Peter, I think we need to step back and look in the mirror. We may not so boldly say, "No, Lord", but we do it in our disobedience to His calling, in not following the teachings of His Word, or holding on to the gunk in our hearts. These are "No Lord" responses just as powerful as if they were spoken out loud.

A good trick that I have is to submit something to God, and then almost immediately I take it back. I am a terrible backseat driver in this way. I say, "Here Lord, I give this to You. Guide me and go before me." No sooner than the words have been uttered, than I am wrestling for control of the situation, not even giving Him a chance to work.

So how do we submit to God?

"You shall walk after the Lord your God and fear Him, and keep His commandments and obey His voice; you shall serve Him and hold fast to Him." (Deuteronomy 13:4) To fear God is to have a reverence and awe for Him.

"But whoever keeps His word, truly the love of God is perfected in him. By this we know that we are in Him. He who says he abides in Him ought himself also to walk just as He walked." (1 John 2:5) When we keep His Word, we are being obedient to Him, and when we are abiding in Jesus, we are allowing Him to live in and through us.

A pastor once joked, "the bumper sticker that used to say, "Jesus is my Co-Pilot" is wrong. He doesn't even want us in the cockpit!" Or in the back seat, or ahead of Him trying to tell Him what He needs to do. As if He didn't already know! We need to let go of the pride, the independent spirit, and come to the Lord in reverence and humility, totally surrendering everything in our lives to Him. What a difference it will make!

REFLECTION TIME

Has there been a time recently when you said no to the Lord? How did that work for you?

_____

_____

_____

_____

Conversely, think of a time when you were obedient to something the Lord was calling you to do. How did He work in the situation?

_____

_____

_____

_____

Meditate on Deuteronomy 13:4. Would you say this has been your approach in your walk with Jesus, or are there parts of this passage that you need to work on?

_____

_____

_____

_____

Write out a prayer asking God to show you where you have been lacking in your obedience, and to help you to truly submit to Him.

_____

_____

_____

_____

Dear Lord:

How we desire to truly call you "Lord". But our flesh gets in the way, and we become like Peter, defying You, delegating You to the role of follower rather than Lord. Please forgive our insubordination. You are the Creator of heaven and earth. So how can we mere mortals act like we know better than You? Please help us, through the power of the Holy Spirit, to surrender everything we have, and everything we are, and to come under total submission to You. We know that this is not a binding control, but it will truly set us free. We thank You and we love You. In Your Holy name we pray, Amen!

CALL TO ACTION!

Marching orders:

Go back to your answer in question #3. Take the passage in Deuteronomy and dissect it. Look at each directive you are given. Write down a practical plan to put those commands into action.

Ready, set, go!

JUST A BUNCH OF SHEEP

(The Good Shepherd)

ON THE WAY TO CHURCH, we pass this crazy, dilapidated barn that looks as if a gust of wind would blow it right over! Sometimes there are a couple of horses in the pasture, and sometimes there are several sheep. One Sunday morning, my sister and I were driving by, and saw one of the sheep standing on the outside of the fence, right along the road. Directly next to it on the other side of the fence the rest of the sheep were huddled together. How it got out in the first place is a mystery, and why they were all standing there together was interesting. Maybe they felt they were comforting the escapee, who knows?

Sheep have some interesting characteristics. First, they have strong herding instincts. They will stay together, and when something frightens them, they band together in large groups. It is harder for the predator to pick them off. Secondly, they frighten easily and will take off together. Or they may wander off on their own, becoming prey.

They also like to play follow the leader and will blindly follow the head sheep even if it is dangerous. There was a true story of how a sheep tried to cross a fifteen-meter deep ravine in Turkey in 2006. Being the followers that they are, the herd of 400 followed the sheep and they all plunged to their death.

One more interesting fact. If a sheep is pregnant, heavy with wool or simply too fat, and it falls over, it cannot get back up on its own. Without aid, it will lay there and die.

When you look at these characteristics of sheep, is it any wonder that God compares us to sheep? Here are some interesting parallels from scripture:

"All we like sheep have gone astray; we have turned, everyone to his own way; and the Lord has laid on Him the iniquity of us all." (Isaiah 53:6) Instead of following our Good Shepherd, we have fallen away, into a life of deception and destruction. But Jesus paid the price for that.

"All the nations will be gathered before Him, and He will separate them one from another, as a shepherd divides his sheep from the goats. And He will set the sheep on His right hand, but the goats on the left. Then the King will say to those on His right hand, 'Come, you blessed of My Father, inherit the kingdom prepared for you from the foundation of the world.'" (Matthew 25:32-34) This is an end times prophecy when Jesus is judging the nations. Good time to be a sheep, right?

"And the Pharisees and scribes complained, saying, 'This Man receives sinners and eats with them.' So He spoke this parable to them, saying: 'What man of you, having a hundred sheep, if he loses one of them, does not leave the ninety-nine in the wilderness, and go after the one which is lost until he finds it? And when he has found it, he lays it on his shoulders, rejoicing. And when he comes home, he calls together his friends and neighbors, saying to them, 'Rejoice with me, for I have found my sheep which was lost!' I say to you that likewise there will be more joy in heaven over one sinner who repents than over ninety-nine just persons who need no repentance." (Luke 15:2-7) This parable is the fulfillment of why Jesus came. He wants no one to perish, so He will go after the lost ones. His purpose was to seek and save the lost. It is a joyous time in heaven when one person is saved!

"I am the good shepherd; and I know My sheep, and am known by My own. As the Father knows Me, even so I know the Father; and I lay down My life for the sheep. And other sheep I have which are not of this fold; them also I must bring, and they will hear My voice; and there will be one flock and one shepherd. As the Father knows Me, even so I know the Father; and I lay down My life for the sheep." (John 10:14-16) Jesus speaks of the intimate relationship that He has with His Father, and that same intimacy He has with

us who are His sheep. If we are abiding in Him, we will know His voice. He came for both the Jews and the Gentiles, and we are all in the same fold.

"I am the good shepherd. The good shepherd gives His life for the sheep. But a hireling, he who is not the shepherd, one who does not own the sheep, sees the wolf coming and leaves the sheep and flees; and the wolf catches the sheep and scatters them. The hireling flees because he is a hireling and does not care about the sheep." (John 10:11-13) A charlatan or a false teacher does not truly care for God's people. They will lead them astray, and then abandon them to the ravenous wolves. This is why it is absolutely essential that we come to recognize the voice of our Savior. It is so easy to be led into a pit.

"Help-I've fallen and I can't get up!" Like the sheep under duress that falls and can't right himself, we can be like that spiritually. But God doesn't leave us in that state. *"The Lord upholds all who fall, and raises up all who are bowed down."* (Psalm 145:14)

Even though we may be like helpless sheep, ripe for the picking by the enemy, we have a Good Shepherd who is watching over us and protecting us. And just as the injured sheep is held close to the shepherd, Jesus holds us close to His heart, loving, protecting, and nurturing us. We are indeed safe in His loving arms. There's no better place to be!

PSALM 23

"The Lord is my shepherd; I shall not want. He makes me to lie down in green pastures; He leads me beside the still waters. He restores my soul; He leads me in the paths of righteousness for His name's sake.

Yea, though I walk through the valley of the shadow of death, I will fear no evil; For You are with me; Your rod and Your staff, they comfort me.

You prepare a table before me in the presence of my enemies; You anoint my head with oil; my cup runs over. Surely goodness and mercy shall follow me all the days of my life; and I will dwell in the house of the Lord forever."

REFLECTION TIME

As we compare the characteristics of sheep to us humans, how do you feel that you are most like them in behavior? Have you been like the sheep that stays close to the Shepherd, or have you found yourself wandering astray lately?

_____

_____

_____

_____

Name some ways how you can draw closer to Jesus and be protected from the ravenous wolves? Be specific in your answer.

_____

_____

_____

_____

Have you studied under a pastor or teacher and felt that they were a hireling or a wolf in sheep's clothing? If so, how did you recognize it, and what course of action did you take?

_____

_____

_____

_____

Write out a prayer asking God to protect you from the snares of the enemy, ask Him to show you how you can draw closer to Him.

_____

_____

_____

Dear Heavenly Father:

We are so much like sheep, helpless against the enemy without Your loving hand of protection. Thank you for being our faithful Shepherd; Who became the sacrificial lamb that was slain for our sins. Help us to know and follow Your voice so we don't get led astray. We love You. In Your strong name, Amen!

CALL TO ACTION!

Marching orders:

At the end of the devotional is Psalm 23. Grab your journal and read through each verse carefully. Take each sentence and dissect it, studying what it means. For example: He is your Shepherd-what does that mean to you? I shall not want- what does the Bible say about His providing our needs? Evaluate each sentence in the psalm in a similar manner. Use a commentary if you have one. Do a word study about shepherd, pastures, restore, etc. Really dive deep into it. Write down your new discoveries. I guarantee this psalm will have a much richer meaning to you when you are finished.

Ready, set, go!

HANDS IN THE KITCHEN

(The Father's Touch)

RECENTLY, A GROUP OF US ladies at church were preparing a meal for the congregation. The church kitchen is equipped with all kinds of tools-spoons, spatulas, mixers, a blender, etc. But the gal in charge simply dug into the dough she was working and said, "The best tool in the kitchen is your hands!" That is very true. The comment came up again when preparing a meal at home. Getting the feel of the dough for bread, or pie crusts takes a certain panache. My mom had a great touch for cooking in that way. In fact, that is how she told us girls how to tell if the dough was worked enough. "Until it feels right!" was a common instruction from her.

Many beautiful things are created from the use of our hands. It is fascinating to watch a potter at his wheel using his hands to create wonderful vessels. He can shape and reshape it as he desires. The mother's hand can give a loving caress to her child. And maybe a swat on the behind when needed. We give a hand up, a handout, a hand clap after a beautiful performance, a handshake of friendship and greeting, we hold hands with our sweetheart as a sign of affection.

As a side-note, it is interesting how God created the opposable thumb to allow for certain tasks that could be very difficult, if not impossible, to do. Humans, of course, have them, but so do primates. Before we go any further, this does NOT support that we are related to monkeys or gorillas, ok? (Although there are some people who act like big apes, but that is not for today's topic!)

Studies show that without the use of your thumb, your hand loses about 40% of its function. Geez, how would you do a thumbs- up to someone? Or do the old hitchhike sign? Or play Seven-Up in school on a rainy day?? (Do they play that anymore?)

God's hand is spoken of in the Bible as well. Here are some examples:

God's hand created all things:

"'Heaven is My throne, and earth is My footstool. What house will you build for Me?' says the Lord. 'Or what is the place of My rest? Has My hand not made all these things?'" (Acts 7:49-50) God has created everything, bigger than any man-made temple.

"When I consider Your heavens, the work of Your fingers, the moon and the stars, which You have ordained, what is man that You are mindful of him, and the son of man that You visit him?" (Psalm 8:3-4) Why would a God so powerful that He created the universe, take time to think of us puny humans? Because He also created us.

"Indeed, My hand has laid the foundation of the earth, and My right hand has stretched out the heavens; when I call to them, they stand up together." (Isaiah 48:13) His right hand stretched out the heavens. Can you even imagine the vastness of that??

"But now, O Lord, You are our Father; we are the clay, and You our potter; and all we are the work of Your hand." (Isaiah 64:8) We are the vessels that God has created. Molded and shaped in His image.

God's hand is upon us:

"Who among all these does not know that the hand of the Lord has done this, in Whose hand is the life of every living thing, and the breath of all mankind?" (Job 12:9-10) Job is lamenting his sufferings, and telling his friends that God holds everything and controls everything. Even our very breath.

"But as for me, I trust in You, O Lord; I say, 'You are my God.' My times are in Your hand; deliver me from the hand of my enemies, and from those who persecute me." (Psalm 31:14-15) Knowing that we are in His hands gives us peace and comfort. He will protect us.

"Both riches and honor come from You, and You reign overall. In Your hand is power and might; in Your hand it is to make great and to give strength to all." (1 Chronicles 29:12) All things come from His mighty hand, whatever it is we need.

His hand protects:

"Fear not, for I am with you; be not dismayed, for I am your God. I will strengthen you, yes, I will help you, I will uphold you with My righteous right hand." (Isaiah 41:10) God will sustain us with His mighty power.

"I have set the Lord always before me; because He is at my right hand, I shall not be moved." (Psalm 16:8) It is a great comfort knowing that God is always with me.

"My Father, who has given them to Me, is greater than all; and no one is able to snatch them out of My Father's hand." (John 10:29) Our salvation is secure in the hand of the Father. No one can take it away from us if we are walking with Him.

The loving hand of God is all powerful; it created the universe which He holds in His palm. The enormity of that is unfathomable. Yet that same mighty hand tenderly holds us and will wipe away every tear in heaven. Truly a loving and gentle Father.

You may not have grown up having an earthly father that loved and nurtured you. It may be hard to understand that gentle loving touch. But know this-God is good, He is kind, and He loves you with an everlasting, unconditional depth of love that cannot be known aside from Him. We are finite beings, He is infinite. Embrace the head knowledge of His love for you, and eventually that will grow into a deep heart knowledge as well!

REFLECTION TIME

Take a moment and try to grasp the vastness of God in light of the universe. Picture everything, the entire solar system, just sitting in the palm of His hand. How does this make you feel?

_____

_____

_____

_____

Given the size of God, how does knowing that He has you, personally, in the palm of His hand, affect your perspective of Him as your loving Father?

_____

_____

_____

_____

Reflect on Isaiah 65:8. How would you want the Potter's hand to mold and shape you in terms of your walk with Him?

_____

_____

_____

_____

Write out a prayer asking God to reveal to you how He has His hand on you. Surrender your ways and ask Him to take total control of the wheel.

_____

_____

_____

_____

Dear Heavenly Father:

When we think of how mighty and powerful You are, it blows our minds to think that even though You can hold the universe in the palm of Your hand, yet You still think of us. Not only do You think of us, but You treat each of us as if we are the only ones in the universe. Your love is so amazing and vast. Help us to surrender to Your hand, as the clay surrenders to the shaping of the potter's wheel. You only have good things for us. Help us to step out in faith and trust that You will do a good work in us. In Your precious name, Amen!

CALL TO ACTION!

Marching orders:

Okay, we are going artistic today! Picture yourself as a lump of clay, soft and pliable, ready to be shaped by the Master's hand. As He rids you of the dry, brittle, unusable pieces, what is He cleaning out? List five things that you would ask Him to help you let go of, so you can be the beautiful vessel that He wants you to be.

Ready, set, go!

OVERCOMER OR JUST OVERCOME?

(Victory in Jesus)

I AM SURE WE ALL have experienced the same thing. Sometimes life just gets too darn overwhelming. We want to throw in the towel. "I'm done!" is the attitude.

Life has a way of bringing us to our knees. Whether it's family dynamics, work issues, or global crises, they have a toll on our emotional well-being. Sometimes you just don't even want to get out of bed. I feel that way every morning when the alarm goes off at 6 a.m. The first words out of my mouth are, "Lord, I can't do this!!" And the response is always is, "Yes you can. Now get up and get going. We have work to do today!"

There are far worse things in life to overcome than my morning grogginess. There are families that are falling apart. Crime seems to be on the rise. People are doing the most horrific things that you never would have dreamed they would do. Just watch the news for ten minutes or scan the newspaper headlines. It is heartbreaking! What is going on out there? I can only imagine how the Lord must feel. He sees the depravity of the entire human race, way beyond my little piece of the world.

Horror stories are as old as time. The first murder recorded in the Bible was in Genesis when Cain killed his own brother Abel because his offering to the Lord was unacceptable (Cain's offering, that is.) Lies, deception, murder, sexual depravity, every sin you can think of has been committed since. And guess who has had his pitchfork right in the middle of things since the very beginning? That old serpent himself, Satan. Yep. He's been deceiving people, leading them astray, bringing them to the brink of destruction. It worked the first time he tried it when he lured Eve to eat the forbidden fruit. He tempted her, he cast doubt on God's word. He used the three-angle approach: the lust of the flesh, the lust of the eyes, and the pride of life. Instead of seeking Adam who was her covering, she bought into Satan's lies and the rest is history. A good lesson here is that the enemy will catch you when you are the most vulnerable. He will push every button he can until he finds your weak spot. Then he goes in for the kill.

Some of our trials we bring on ourselves. We go where we shouldn't go, we fall for the lie that just one time won't matter, or I'm not hurting anyone else, so it's my business. Wrong! We are not on this earth alone. Every action we take has an impact on others around us, whether we believe it or not.

Then there are those trials that are beyond our control. The company is downsizing and we are getting laid off, the car broke down, there was a cancer diagnosis. Truly difficult things that can totally overwhelm us. And we are overcome by our circumstances.

God does not want us living in a state of self-defeat. He wants us to live in victory. His victory. Here are some tools for overcoming:

"And He said to me, 'My grace is sufficient for you, for My strength is made perfect in weakness.' Therefore, most gladly I will rather boast in my infirmities, that the power of Christ may rest upon me." (2 Corinthians 12:9) This is a case where God gives the strength to get through the trial. Paul had prayed three times for his affliction to be removed. But God used the affliction for His purposes and gave Paul the strength to endure and carry on.

"But he who endures to the end shall be saved." (Matthew 24:13) A believer will endure trials through the power of the Holy Spirit.

"For whatever is born of God overcomes the world. And this is the victory that has overcome the world—our faith. Who is he who overcomes the world, but he who believes that Jesus is the Son of God?" (1 John 5:4-5) The tool here for overcoming is faith. Not faith that (fill in the blank) but faith that Jesus is the Son of God. Period.

"Therefore, submit to God. Resist the devil and he will flee from you." (James 4:7). This is kind of a no-brainer. Stay away from the temptation! If you have a drinking problem, stay out of the bars. If you are tempted with pornography, put a filter on your computer that blocks it. Do practical things to thwart the enemy, after you have submitted the problem to the Lord.

"These things I have spoken to you, that in Me you may have peace. In the world you will have tribulation; but be of good cheer, I have overcome the world." (John 16:33) We can have peace despite our circumstances, because Jesus overcame sin and death. He fought and won the battle for us.

"Yet in all these things we are more than conquerors through Him who loved us. For I am persuaded that neither death nor life, nor angels nor principalities nor powers, nor things present nor things to come, nor height nor depth, nor any other created thing, shall be able to separate us from the love of God which is in Christ Jesus our Lord." (Romans 8:37-39) We have the ability to conquer anything that life and the enemy throws at us because we have the power to be victorious through the love of Jesus Christ. And here is why:

"You are of God, little children, and have overcome them, because He who is in you is greater than he who is in the world." (1 John 4:4)

So take heart, we can be overcomers through the power of Jesus Christ living in us. But remember, we don't have to take on the battle because:

The Lord will fight for you, and you shall hold your peace." (Exodus 14:14) The Israelites were afraid they were going to die, and Moses gave them this encouragement. Sometimes we need to just get out of God's way, stand back and let Him fight the battle.

"Do not be afraid nor dismayed because of this great multitude, for the battle is not yours, but God's." (2 Chronicles 20:15b) Our trials and tribulations may look like giants in our eyes, but to God they are tiny little grasshoppers. And as God said to Jeremiah, *"Behold, I am the Lord, the God of all flesh. Is there anything too hard for Me?"* (Jeremiah 32:27) I think the answer is clear on that one!

REFLECTION TIME

Life can certainly throw us for a loop. Think of a recent time when you were feeling overwhelmed by a trial. How did the Lord see you through it?

_____

_____

_____

_____

Think of a time when you struggled through something without seeking the Lord. How did you handle it, and what do you think you would have done differently if you had sought the Lord?

_____

_____

_____

_____

Reflect on Romans 8:27-39. How does this passage give you comfort when you are going through a difficult time?

_____

_____

_____

_____

Write out a prayer, asking God to help you through a current trial, or thank Him for seeing you through a past one.

_____

_____

_____

_____

Dear Heavenly Father:

Thank You, Lord, that we don't have to face the trials and tribulations of this world alone. Thank You that we have You to fight our battles, to guard and protect us as we traverse the troubled waters of life. Help us to remember to call out to You, and to relinquish our hold on these problems. Otherwise, they are going to pull us down like an anchor. But You, Lord, are our anchor in the storm. And because of Your love for us, we are indeed more than conquerors, and that we don't fight FOR victory, we fight FROM victory. You have already won the battle. Thank You! In Your strong name, Amen!

CALL TO ACTION!

Marching orders:

"For though we walk in the flesh, we do not war according to the flesh. For the weapons of our warfare are not carnal but mighty in God for pulling down strongholds, casting down arguments and every high thing that exalts itself against the knowledge of God, bringing every thought into captivity to the obedience of Christ." (2 Corinthians 10:3-5)

Alright, warriors! We are going to conquer the world today. But we are not going to use carnal weapons of warfare, but the weapons of spiritual warfare. Today, you are being called to engage in the war using prayer as your weapon. I want you to choose two things that you are going to commit to prayer for the next seven days (longer would be better). You will virtually march around these "walls of Jericho" (read Joshua 6 if you don't know the story) tear down the walls of sin. Choose something or someone personal in your own world, and something of a broader scope.

Remember, the greatest battles are fought on our knees!

Ready, set, go!

VANITY, VANITY
(How God Sees Us)

FLIP THROUGH ANY MAGAZINE, AND you are inundated with ads picturing (no doubt airbrushed) beautiful, healthy people. The promise is that if you use their product, you can look like them. Beautiful, flowing hair, rippling muscles, flawless skin. Outer beauty is the measuring stick we are put up against.

People spend countless hours at the gym trying to lose weight, or get bulging biceps and washboard abs. They pop prescriptions like they were candy. But have you read all the side effects?? They are worse than the disease!

Here are some mind-boggling numbers for you in the global markets of these industries for various recent years annually:

Fitness industry: $100 Billion
Organic food market: $110 billion
Beauty industry: $545 Billion
Fast food market: $570 Billion
Big Pharma market: $937 Billion

No doubt you are wondering why we are discussing this in a devotional about Jesus. I am getting to my point, trust me.

Look at the trend of the markets. The ones where we actually do things for ourselves that are healthiest, have the lowest revenue. The middle one is artificial and topical. But notice the bottom two. Fast food and pharmacy. They seem to go hand in hand, don't they? The trend looks like this: I would rather eat my unhealthy fast food and take meds to fix the problems they cause, or slap on some war paint to cover flaws, over putting in a little effort to take care of my body. It just seems easier that way, doesn't it?

But God has a different perspective about beauty. While man is concerned with the outer appearance, God looks at the beauty that is inside.

"Do not let your adornment be merely outward—arranging the hair, wearing gold, or putting on fine apparel— rather let it be the hidden person of the heart, with the incorruptible beauty of a gentle and quiet spirit, which is very precious in the sight of God." (1 Peter 3:3-4) God sees the inner beauty of our spirit as far more precious than our outward adornment.

"Therefore, we do not lose heart. Even though our outward man is perishing, yet the inward man is being renewed day by day." (2 Corinthians 4:16) The physical body is wearing down as we age. And don't we know that! But God sends a fresh supply of what we need in our spirit.

"I will praise You, for I am fearfully and wonderfully made; marvelous are Your works, and that my soul knows very well." (Psalm 139:14) So many of us have a sell-image issue. But we are made in His image, and are miraculous, beautiful works of art.

"In like manner also, that the women adorn themselves in modest apparel, with propriety and moderation, not with braided hair or gold or pearls or costly clothing, but, which is proper for women professing godliness, with good works." (1 Timothy 2:9-10) A Godly woman does not parade herself around, deliberately drawing attention to her outer appearance.

"But the Lord said to Samuel, 'Do not look at his appearance or at his physical stature, because I have refused him. For the Lord does not see as man sees; for man looks at the outward appearance, but the Lord looks at the heart.'"

(1 Samuel 16:7) We could look like Quasimodo, but if we have a heart that follows Jesus, we are beautiful in God's eyes.

"Charm is deceitful and beauty is passing, but a woman who fears the Lord, she shall be praised." (Proverbs 31:30) A Godly woman is beautiful at any age.

Paul tells us that we are to present our bodies as a living sacrifice, holy and acceptable to the Lord. Like everything He gives us, we are to be good stewards of it. But, as human nature tends to do, we can go overboard. We need to be good stewards and take care of ourselves. But our bodies can become our idols. I heard a pastor quip once, when talking about the diet and exercise fads: "Why do we work so hard to stay out of the place we say we all want to go to?" (Meaning prolonging our lives) Interestingly, he was quite a heavy man…

We have got to be so careful about not buying into what society tells us. That our self-worth is tied up in appearances. Have you ever seen a very physically attractive woman, but when she opens her mouth to speak, ugly vile words come out? She may be beautiful on the outside, but inside there is a hot mess. But thankfully Jesus can take that mess, clean it out and wash us clean. He will give us a new heart, one that will radiate beauty. This will transform us, and we will be beautiful vessels reflecting Jesus. There's no amount of makeup that can do that!

Remember this: You are beautifully and uniquely made by God. He chose your nose, eye color, skin tone, height and all the many other features that make up you. Embrace your uniqueness and be that beautiful woman or man of God He designed you to be.

REFLECTION TIME

Have you wrestled with the signals from the world that we are to be thin, beautiful, flawless human beings to have value in this world? How have you reconciled that with what God says-that you are a beautiful creation?

_____

_____

_____

_____

What are some things that you can change in your heart that would reflect inner beauty in your appearance? How would that show itself outwardly?

_____

_____

_____

_____

Meditate on Proverbs 31:30. How does inner beauty transcend wrinkles and age spots and all those wonderful things that come with age?

_____

_____

_____

_____

Write out a prayer thanking God for making you the way He did. Ask Him to show you what He thinks is beautiful about you that you don't notice.

_____

_____

_____

_____

Dear Heavenly Father:

Thank You that You love us no matter how we look on the outside. Thank You that You look to the inner man or woman for beauty. We can get so easily caught up in what the world defines as beauty, that we forget we are not here to please the world, but to please You. Forgive us when we get wrapped up in our appearance. It is true that we are to be good stewards of all that You give us, which includes our health and our appearance. Help us to find that perfect balance between the two. Let our words and our actions reflect Your beauty in everything we say or do. In Your precious name, Amen!

CALL TO ACTION!

Marching orders:

Time for a self-image inner beauty makeover!

It is hard to reconcile outer beauty that the world judges us on, and inner beauty that God sees. Get your journal out, and list five things you don't like about your appearance. Give those over to God and ask Him to show you where you are truly beautiful. Then, list five things about your heart that is not pleasing to God and ask Him to show you how to change them.

That is a swing of ten beauty marks. And it didn't cost a penny. Take that, L'Oréal!

Ready, set, go!

BRINGING IT ALL TOGETHER

(It's All About Jesus)

TODAY'S DEVOTIONAL IS A SUMMARY of everything we have learned about Jesus in both books of "It's All About Jesus The Living Word". My hope and prayer is that you were able to relate to the stories. That through thoughtful prayer and study, the scriptures became more meaningful and personal to you. And through the questions, you were challenged to think about how the scriptures applied.

When we look at God's Word, it is important to understand that the entire book, from Genesis 1 to Revelation 22 is all about Jesus. It is His story.

Augustine was quoted as saying this: "The Old Testament is the New Testament concealed. The New Testament is the Old Testament revealed."

Regarding the Old Testament (which was the law):

"For the law, having a shadow of the good things to come, and not the very image of the things, can never with these same sacrifices, which they offer continually year by year, make those who approach perfect." (Hebrews 10:1)

In other words, the annual animal sacrifices were never enough to completely atone for sin. The shadow of good things to come refers to the Person of Jesus Christ, whose sacrifice and the shedding of innocent blood was the only way that we can become perfect.

There are over 100 Old Testament prophecies regarding Jesus that was fulfilled in the New Testament.

Regarding the New Testament (the doctrine of grace)

"Then He said to them, 'O foolish ones, and slow of heart to believe in all that the prophets have spoken! Ought not the Christ to have suffered these things and to enter into His glory?' And beginning at Moses and all the Prophets, He expounded to them in all the Scriptures the things concerning Himself." (Luke 24:25-27)

Jesus, on the road to Emmaus, was explaining to two men, the entire gospel, going back to Moses. This demonstrates that the Old Testament is full of references to Jesus.

As we tackled many topics, we discovered that passages from all over the Bible can be found on just about any topic you can think of. Whether it be hope, fear, grace, obedience, sin, gossip, forgiveness, going deeper in the Word, we discovered nuggets all along the way.

As we continue to press in to Jesus, learn of His Word, it is important to call on the whole counsel of God's Word. It is vital to our spiritual health.

"In the beginning was the Word, and the Word was with God, and the Word was God. He was in the beginning with God. All things were made through Him, and without Him nothing was made that was made. In Him was life, and the life was the light of men. And the light shines in the darkness, and the darkness did not comprehend it." (John 1:1-5) Jesus existed from all eternity. He did not have a beginning, He dwelt with God, He WAS God.

Seeing that Jesus IS the Word, it shows that we need to learn all of it. Here are some passages about the Word:

"For the word of God is living and powerful, and sharper than any two-edged sword, piercing even to the division of soul and spirit, and of joints

and marrow, and is a discerner of the thoughts and intents of the heart."
(Hebrews 4:12) The Word gives us discernment and understanding that we
cannot otherwise have.

*"All Scripture is given by inspiration of God, and is profitable for doctrine, or
reproof, for correction, for instruction in righteousness, that the man of God
may be complete, thoroughly equipped for every good work."* (2 Timothy
3:16-17) They were written by man, but under the inspiration of the Holy
Spirit. You can trust that God oversaw the entire process!

*"Therefore, whoever hears these sayings of Mine, and does them, I will liken
him to a wise man who built his house on the rock"* (Matthew 7:24) When we
hear and obey the Word, we are building our foundation on the Rock-Jesus!

*"And it happened, as He spoke these things, that a certain woman from the
crowd raised her voice and said to Him, "Blessed is the womb that bore You,
and the breasts which nursed You! But He said, "More than that, blessed are
those who hear the word of God and keep it!"* (Luke 11:28) Jesus was speaking
of our spiritual relationship being more important than human relationships.

In closing, to truly live out the Christian life, we need to read the Word,
understand it, and apply it. In any situation we may face, our first response
should always be, "What does Jesus have to say about it?" As we learn it,
we will be able to draw from it. The Holy Spirit will aid us in bringing it to
remembrance. It will also help us to discern false teachings, cults, and devious
tactics of the enemy.

"Your word I have hidden in my heart, that I might not sin against You."

(Psalm 119:11) By learning His Word, we are spiritually stronger, and more
able to avoid sinful behaviors.

*"But Simon Peter answered Him, 'Lord, to whom shall we go? You have the
words of eternal life. Also, we have come to believe and know that You are
the Christ, the Son of the living God.'"* (John 6:68) No better words came out

of the mouth of Peter. He had the advantage of being in the physical presence of Jesus. We cannot do this, so we have the next best thing. The Living Word, 66 books-all about Jesus! We need to keep in mind that the two testaments cannot be separated, because they are so beautifully connected to our Lord and Savior, the Author and Finisher of our faith, from Genesis to Revelation. Amazing!

REFLECTION TIME

Think about your journey through the devotionals. How has learning God's Word increased your faith?

_____

_____

_____

_____

Flip through the pages of the devotional book. Is there one particular day that spoke to you more than the others? How did it touch you?

_____

_____

_____

_____

Review John 6:68. How has God's Word kept you focused on your relationship with Jesus and to increase your belief in Him?

_____

_____

_____

_____

Write out a prayer, thanking God for His Word, and the power of it in your life.

_____

_____

_____

_____

_____

Dear Heavenly Father:

Thank You for the gift of Your word. Thank You that everything we need to navigate this life is found in the pages of the Bible. Help us to always seek You first for direction, comfort, peace, strength-all which can be found as we study Your word. Help us have a passion for it, understanding of it through the power of the Holy Spirit. Thank You for loving us, and giving Your life for us. One day we will see You face to face, and Your Word will truly be alive for us. In Your name, Amen!

CALL TO ACTION!

Marching orders:

OK, this is a tall order. Psalm 119, which has 176 verses, is your homework. This Psalm is all about God's Word. It is divided into 8-verse sections. Going through each section, study what it says about the Word. Note how many times it's referenced. Keywords- word, precept, law, statutes, testament, ways are all descriptions of the Word.

When you have completed it, note the common threads between each section. Choose five verses that you want to commit to memory.

Ready, set, go!

CONCLUSION

YOU ARE PROBABLY WONDERING, WHAT'S next on the agenda? Hopefully you have completed both volumes of "IT'S ALL ABOUT JESUS THE LIVING WORD". (If not, go now and grab volume 1). Go back and review some of the devotionals that touched you. It's always good to revisit scriptures. If you haven't dug into the passages, now is a good time to go back and do that. Have you answered all the questions thoughtfully?

COMING SOON!

I am excited to announce that in early Spring of 2020, we will start a new series. Books 3 and 4 of the "IT'S ALL ABOUT JESUS THE LIVING WORD" Series will delve into various Bible stories. We will use the same devotional format. Turn the page for a sneak peek:

A WHALE OF A TALE – Jonah's Disobedience

For updates on release dates and special deals, please join our Facebook group**:**

ITS ALL ABOUT JESUS

God bless you, and we will see you soon!

A WHALE OF A TALE

(Jonah's Disobedience)

I'M SURE YOU ARE ALL familiar with the story of Jonah. But here's a recap, just in case you have forgotten. He was called to sail to Nineveh, a city corrupt with sin. God wanted him to preach the message of repentance. Jonah didn't want to do this, so he sailed in the opposite direction. A fierce storm came upon the boat, and he admitted to the crew that it was his fault and they should throw him overboard. They liked this idea and did just that.

"Now the Lord had prepared a great fish to swallow Jonah. And Jonah was in the belly of the fish three days and three nights." (Jonah 1:17). A couple of things to note here. First, the Lord "had" prepared a great fish. This indicates to me that He knew in advance what Jonah was going to do. He didn't do it in response to Jonah's actions. Secondly, it is called a "great fish". Much debate and study has gone into this as to what type of fish this was. The argument against it being a whale is that whales are mammals, not fish. The argument for it being a whale is the size. Remember, Jonah was swallowed whole. For a full-grown man to be able to fit inside a fish it has got to be huge. But either way, let's not lose sight of the fact that God can do anything.

Back to the story. After three days and nights in the belly of this great fish, the Lord spoke to it, and it vomited Jonah out. Can you imagine the stench?? I gag on the smell of fish in general. He must have reeked beyond belief!

Here's some things that blow my mind about his time in the belly. First, in chapter 2 it says AFTER three days and nights, he prayed to the Lord. I don't know about you, but I would have been praying all the way down the gullet! "Help me Lord!" would have been my cry. Then a few verses of Jonah's lament about his situation. It says *then* he remembered the Lord. Again, what took you so long, buddy?

Wrapping up the story, after he was vomited out and smelling like a sewer, he delivered his message from God. The entire city repented. Time for celebration and praise to God from the fish man, right? Nope! The only party Jonah threw was a pity party. He didn't like the outcome.

⸙

This is an interesting study into human nature. Oftentimes as Christians, we give a good talk about how we love others and desire them to be saved. But deep down, if we are honest, there's those who we feel don't deserve forgiveness and should rot in hell for eternity. Granted, there are some incredibly evil people out there. But believe it or not, Christ died for them as well, and they have the same opportunity to repent and be saved as we do. We cannot be walking around being junior holy spirits. That's not our job.

Another point here is the consequences of disobedience. That must have been quite an ordeal for Jonah those three days. And what about the people on the boat that he got into? They were put in real jeopardy because of Jonah's rebellion. Proof that our actions affect other people.

Thirdly, God accomplished His will, using Jonah as planned. Granted, Jonah went kicking and screaming through the entire process, and because of his attitude, missed out on the blessing of seeing an entire city repent. If our hearts are truly aligned with God's we should be doing spiritual cartwheels in rejoice!

The story doesn't tell us why Jonah had such a hatred for these people. But this was his reaction when God saved the city from destruction: ***"But it displeased***

Jonah exceedingly, and he became angry. So he prayed to the Lord, and said, 'Ah, Lord, was not this what I said when I was still in my country? Therefore I fled previously to Tarshish; for I know that You are a gracious and merciful God, slow to anger and abundant in lovingkindness, One who relents from doing harm.' "(Jonah 4:1-2)

I find this very interesting, and so true to human nature. He asked for, and received, mercy and grace from God when he was in the middle of his crisis. God delivered him. But he was angry when the Ninevites were given the same grace and forgiveness. How often we want mercy for us, but judgment for the other guy. Why do we esteem ourselves better than others? Why are we so special? As is usually the case, our hearts and attitudes are in direct conflict with what God wants from us.

"Let nothing be done through selfish ambition or conceit, but in lowliness of mind let each esteem others better than himself." (Philippians 2:3).

None of us are deserving of forgiveness. Isaiah refers to our righteousness as to being like filthy rags. Dirty, smelly, rotten. Much like Jonah, before he repented of his behavior. But God chose to forgive him and allow him to carry out his assignment. But also, like Jonah, once the crisis was over, we can so easily revert to our own selfish, self-centered attitudes. Let's not be like that, ok?

REFLECTION TIME

Do you have a Jonah experience? Think of a time you openly rebelled against a command from the Lord! What was the outcome?

_____

_____

_____

_____

What do you think are some ways that being disobedient to God can cost us?

_____

_____

_____

_____

Mediate on Philippians 2:3. How does this scripture speak to you? Think of a recent time when you did something out of humility.

_____

_____

_____

_____

Write out a prayer, asking God to forgive you for a disobedient heart, and to desire to do His will.

_____

_____

_____

_____

_____

Dear Heavenly Father:

God, give us clean hands and pure hearts. Remove the stench of rebellion from us. And let us wear the sweet aroma of Jesus that draws people to you. Show us Your ways and desires for our lives and help us to want to walk in them gladly. In Your name, Amen!

CALL TO ACTION!

Marching orders:

Grab your journal. Write down five incidences where you have demonstrated disobedience to the Lord. What did you do, or not do, and if you had a do-over, what would He have you do differently?

Ready, set, go!

ABOUT THE AUTHOR

Deborah Bedson is a native of Southern California. Desiring a more rural lifestyle, she moved to North Washington State in 2015, where she fell in love with the beauty of God's creation. Time spent working in the Christian retail industry gave her a love for spreading the Word of God. After many encouraging words from family and friends to write (and much prayer about how to do this), "It's All About Jesus-the Living Word" was born. It is her prayer that the reader will develop a deeper, more meaningful connection to God.

For related resources, check out Deborah's website:

https://its-all-about-jesus-the-living-word.com/

email: itsallaboutjesusthelivingword@gmail.com

Please join us at our private Facebook group page:

ITS ALL ABOUT JESUS THE LIVING WORD

THANK YOU

FOR READING MY BOOK!

I really appreciate all of your feedback,
And I love hearing what you have to say.

I need your input to make the next version
Of this book and my future books better.

Pleas leave me an honest review on Amazon.com
Letting me know what you thought of the book.

Thanks again!

Deborah Bedson

Made in the USA
Monee, IL
25 January 2020